D0049564

UNPACKING THE BOXES

Unpacking the Boxes

A Memoir of a Life in Poetry

Donald Hall

Houghton Mifflin Company

BOSTON · NEW YORK

2008

For information about permission to reproduce selections from this
book, write to Permissions, Houghton Mifflin Company,
215 Park Avenue South, New York, New York 10003.

www.houghtonmifflinbooks.com

Library of Congress Cataloging-in-Publication Data

Hall, Donald, date.
Unpacking the boxes : a memoir of a life in poetry / Donald Hall.
p. cm.
ISBN: 978-0-618-99065-8
1. Hall, Donald, date. 2. Poets, American—20th century—Biography.
3. Poets laureate—United States. 4. Authorship. I. Title.
PS3515.A3152Z478 2008
811'.54—dc22
[B]   2008004624

Book design by Anne Chalmers
Typeface: Filosofia

Printed in the United States of America

DOC 10 9 8 7 6 5 4 3 2 1

Lines from "Elegy Just in Case" by John Ciardi are reprinted with the permission
of Miller Williams, Literary Executor, the Estate of John Ciardi.
The last stanza of "Afternoon at MacDowell" by Jane Kenyon, copyright © 2004,
the Estate of Jane Kenyon, are reprinted from *Collected Poems* with the permission
of Graywolf Press, St. Paul, Minnesota.

In Memory of Liam Rector

Contents

UNPACKING THE

BOXES

Domains

AT FOURTEEN I DECIDED to spend my life writing poetry, which is what I have done. My parents supported my desire, or at least did not attempt to dissuade me. My father hated his work, and it was his passion that I should do what I wanted to do. My mother was prevented by her gender and her era (born 1903) from exercising her intense aimless ambition, which settled on me. They worried how I would make a living at poetry, but would not pressure me to join the prosperous family business, the Brock-Hall Dairy in Connecticut, where my father added columns of figures from Monday into Saturday. Their support was affectionate, passive, and generous. Beginning when I was a freshman in high school, they gave me for Christmas and birthdays the many books of poetry I listed for them.

Why did I come to poetry at such an age? A few years ago in Nebraska, talking about my beginnings to high school students, I told about wanting to write because I loved Poe and Keats, later Eliot and Yeats. A skeptical boy asked, "Didn't you do it to pick up chicks?" "Yes!" I answered. "How could I forget?" In the absence of athletic skill, I found that poetry attracted at least the arty girls if not the cheerleaders. Ambition exists to provide avenue for the libido. This notion begets another, less flattering to the peacock male ego: Maybe all women are the one woman, and everything gets done to woo Mom.

My mother died at ninety, in 1994, while my wife Jane Kenyon was sick. I emptied my mother's house, and a moving van left seventy or eighty boxes at our house and at a cottage we owned down the road. For a long time I could not open them. Three years after Jane died my assistant Kendel Currier moved into the cottage and helped me unpack the boxes. Most of the books would go to the library at the University of New Hampshire. From other boxes my childhood rose like a smoke of moths: a 78 of Connee Boswell singing "The Kerry Dance"; all the letters I ever wrote my father and mother; photographs of my young parents on the boardwalk at Atlantic City; my father's colorless Kodachromes of Long Island Sound; snapshots of cats dead for fifty years; model airplanes and toy cars and a Boy Scout manual, a baseball, and a baseball glove with its oiled pocket chewed by mice. I felt the shock and exultation of exhumation.

For weeks I unpacked the boxes, releasing the beginning decades of a life that was concluding its seventh: There were reams of manuscript, a thousand poems, novels I wrote at seventeen and nineteen; high school magazines with my poems and stories—the antique tracks of poetry and ambition. I found a high school theme called "The Wild Heifers." I found a verse play called *The Folly of Existence*. The unpacked boxes laid out my childhood and adolescence as if they assembled a model train, Lionel Standard Gauge, complete with a miniature village set beside the tracks, a hill for the train to tunnel through, a semaphore, mirror glass for a pond. I recollected earliest childhood, seeing a solemn child, three years old. He looks lonely, discontent, bored. At the height of summer he stands, wearing shorts with socks sliding down ankles over indistinct shoes, holding an indistinct toy beside a gray clapboard house, in heat and dust, under a sun that will not relent. The image resembles a black-and-white photograph, but I don't believe it's a remembered snapshot. In family photographs Donnie is spiffed up with his hair combed and water-slicked, his arms stiff at his sides. Donnie was spiffed up and photographed many times: not merely an only child but an only grandchild. Perhaps I was discontent as the focus of the family lens, standing under a sun of singular attention and expectation.

In childhood nothing happened. Born in 1928 as Mickey Mouse was—Thomas Hardy died that year—I breathed the air of the Great Depression. Men stood on street corners selling apples and pencils; tramps came to the back door—but my father had a secure job. My mother and father had married on September 10, 1927, and rented the second floor of a house on Coram Street near Lake Whitney in a neighborhood of Hamden, Connecticut, that developers called Spring Glen. Although my mother had been told that she was unlikely to bear a child, I was born a year and ten days after the wedding. When I was one, my parents moved, renting a small house two miles away in another part of Hamden called Whitneyville, originally the site of housing that Eli Whitney made for workers at his gun factory. (A dam at the end of Lake Whitney supplied waterpower.) By the time my father was born, in 1903, near Whitney Avenue, Whitney's village was becoming a New Haven suburb, and soon a trolley line ran four miles to the city's green. The family business thrived a few blocks from our Winette Street house. The Brock-Hall Dairy's horses and wagons delivered milk seven days a week to the back doors of New Haven and its suburbs. Hamden was my father's place, far from my mother's rural New Hampshire. Sometimes my grandmother Kate visited from the farm, a day's journey by train. My grandfather Wesley came rarely; he needed to stay home and tend to the animals. The generations were close in age: My parents were twenty-five when I was born, and Kate was only twenty-five years older.

Nothing happened. Some stories of childhood are tales that grown-ups repeated. I must have been three when I pulled the carrot, and my mother told everyone what Donnie did. She kept a vegetable garden at the bottom of the back yard, and every night before supper she took me with her to pull a fresh carrot for my supper. One evening I walked into the kitchen, a little early, holding my carrot of exemplary intelligence. Memory is stronger when it recalls transgression. I played with a neighbor boy while a repairman worked on the kitchen refrigerator, which had a white coil at its top. The repairman's dented Model T, cut down to a pickup, stood beside the kitchen door on two narrow strips of breaking-apart cement. My playmate and I lifted chunks of concrete onto the pickup's bed. My mother, peeking out the screen door, issued a reprimand, and my friend and I set to undo the crime. I stood in the truck bed lifting chunks down to my accomplice, who wore an Indian headdress. I stood above the boy looking down on his head surrounded by feathers, and carefully dropped a large lump of concrete onto his skull. Oh, the bliss of targeting a head circled by feathers! He howled and ran home; I was sent to my room.

Nothing happened. I was small when I wandered a block or two up Augur Street, and sideways into one of the short blocks that paralleled Winette, with no notion of how to get home. Desolation. A tender deliveryman in a red truck returned me to my distraught mother. When I was four I saw my first nude female body. The three-year-old daughter of friends of my parents, who also lived on Winette, came dashing naked out of her house as I walked up the street. I remember my wicked joy as I watched a flustered grandmother run from the house and grab Molly back into privacy. License and rapture began with this vision. My father's parents lived nearby. After a blizzard, my grandfather Henry Hall, who loved horses, had his picture in the *New Haven Register* because he saddled up and delivered Brock-Hall milk to customers with babies. (He kept a saddle horse with the milk-truck workhorses in the dairy's long stable.) Yet, Henry and Augusta were frightening figures to me—because they were frightening to my parents. Their house was always dark; it felt like held breath. When we visited them, often on Sundays, I picked up my parents' anxiety. Would my mother be mocked for her New Hampshire accent? Would my father be found wanting, and be chewed by his father's sarcasm? My father was first child of Henry the self-made man, known at the dairy as H.F., who left school after fifth grade and by hard, honest work built up a business. My father was raised to understand that he could never do anything right, and when he died at fifty-two still labored in vain for his father's approval. On the other hand, my mother grew up eldest of three girls—she was forever the older sister; even in her eighties she was older sister to the universe—on a farm in rural New Hampshire, oil lamps and church Sundays and an outhouse with five graduated holes. Brought together by the chance of college, in their backgrounds my parents were diverse. Hamden was alien in its gentility and sophistication, and my mother felt intimidated by the manners and mores of Whitneyville and Spring

Glen. If she pronounced "Coca-Cola" as "Coker-Coaler," she was teased. Her mother-in-law Augusta had the habit, at our house, of trailing a white-gloved finger across the ledge invisible on top of a doorjamb, then displaying a digit of dust. Doubtless Augusta, daughter of unschooled German immigrants, had needed to establish her own credentials.

Nevertheless, my mother tried to do everything as it should be done. She embraced Hamden's suburban culture with the appearance of enthusiasm. When she rode the trolley into New Haven, to shop at Malley's or Shartenberg's, she wore a hat, a veil, and gloves. My father earned thirty-five dollars a week, yet they spent five of the dollars to hire a full-time maid. Aggie (for Agnes) O'Brien, ten years younger than my parents, was not servile. She sat at the kitchen table with my mother, smoking cigarettes and chatting. I loved Aggie and cuddled with her, listening to her favorite radio programs. She agreed to wait, to marry me when I caught up with her. When my mother felt required to put Aggie in a black dress and black stockings with a white apron, like the French maid in the play, Aggie turned sullen. My mother costumed Aggie when she invited three women friends for bridge in the afternoon. I peeked as the women arrived, one with a fur piece, all lipsticked and powdered, smelling of perfume, three wives in their late twenties or early thirties, wearing dresses and girdles, wearing silk stockings and fancy shoes, wearing hats with veils: tea, cookies, and cakes.

Although my mother struggled to conform to Hamden, she returned as often as she could to the New Hampshire farm where she grew up, and to my maternal grandparents. Before I started school, she took me with her by train, and quickly I came to love the farm more than I loved Hamden's blocks of six-room houses. Preferring the one place to the other was choosing my mother over my father. A suburban child, I was all the more Connecticut in preferring rural New Hampshire. (Real New Hampshirites don't prefer the state; they are it.) My conflict of geographies—two parents, two cultures—shaped the devices and desires of my heart. It wasn't until I was fifty, and had moved to the empty maternal New Hampshire farmhouse for good, that I understood how assiduously my mother had determined my preference. Upstairs, Kate kept a fold-down desk of treasures, and there I found my mother's penny postcard, forty-eight years earlier addressed to Kate and Wesley from Connecticut. My mother wrote after she and I had returned to Hamden from a visit: "Donnie's been shouting 'Gale, Gale'"—which was the name of the Boston and Maine depot a mile from the farm—"and then saying 'Oh, there's Grampa.' He plays 'Go to New Hampshire on the choo-choo train.'"

Kate Wells was a fierce conservative of family, farm, and church. Nothing in this house was thrown away; everything connected to the departed was preserved and cherished. Kate had been the beloved youngest child of Ben and Lucy Keneston, born when her father was fifty-two. She loved them back, and would never part with their detritus. The family's history is preserved in this house—in mothholed sweaters, fragile quilts, broken chairs, mildewed books—like Lenin in his tomb. Kate lamented that her eldest daughter had settled so far away, as I might complain if my son relocated with the grandchildren to Ulan Bator. My mother Lucy felt mildly treacherous because she had abandoned her family, even as she tried to adapt to Hamden: Automobiles, cigarettes, Scotch whiskey, bridge, and restaurants were none of them available or acceptable back home. As a propitiatory donation she gave my soul to New Hampshire, to house and landscape, family and culture. My grandparents accepted the gift, and my grandmother continued to cherish it into her nineties. I spent most of my young summers on the farm, in love with my grandparents and the disappearing countryside. I wrote my first prose book about these summers, *String Too Short to Be Saved*. I married; I provided Kate two great-grandchildren. When I lived and taught in Michigan, I returned every summer for a few days to the farm and the old woman who still kept sheep. In her nineties she asked me if, when I was far away and spoke of this place, I called it "home."

From Connecticut we visited New Hampshire off and on all year. Just before Christmas and in August, my father drove the family to the farm in the Studebaker. Otherwise, my mother and I took the train, climbing into the great steel cars that puffed steam at the New Haven station, sitting at a window on the right side of the aisle to look out on seagulls and oyster flats during our journey. The long links of our train aimed for the hive of enormous South Station in Boston, hub of the Hub. A man came through the car hawking magazines, cigarettes, chewing gum, candy, and cheese sandwiches. We were already provisioned. My mother opened the shoebox before New London, Connecticut—exposing a chest (ingots and gold coins) of half sandwiches on decrusted soft bread, each in its own waxed-paper jacket: cream cheese and pineapple, egg salad, chopped ham and pickle; also a stuffed deviled egg; also a frosted cupcake. The New York,

New Haven, and Hartford slid past the Connecticut shore, up
along Rhode Island to Boston, where we alighted to take a taxi
to North Station. The yellow cab beeped through Boston traffic.
The station pointing north was smaller, less busy, not so shiny
as South Station. From here we set out on our journey backward
in time. The locomotive was old, the cars rickety, cloth seat covers ripped and sewed together. The train journeyed through suburbs for half an hour, then reached open country. I looked from
my window seat at herds of Holsteins grazing in pastures among
the shut-down mill towns (shoes, textiles) north of Boston. The
conductor called out "Lowell," "Lawrence," "Nashua," "Manchester" at the brick stops between farmlands. The conductor
was old, with a bright red face and a white handkerchief tucked
between his neckskin and his loose collar. When he called out
"Concord"—"Con-CUD"—we were coming close. "Boscawen"
was pronounced "Bahs-COIN." (For years I assumed it an Indian
word but it is Cornish, the name of an English admiral who fought
in the French and Indian War. The resolution of that war opened
this part of New Hampshire to settlement from Massachusetts.)
"Frank-LIN." (Ben Franklin wasn't born there but Daniel Web-
ster was, and it was to Franklin that my mother and her sisters
journeyed by train to high school, as their mother had done before them.) "Halcyon" was the depot at East Andover, followed by
the town of Andover, the hamlet of Potter Place, and at last West
Andover where the depot was "Gale." My grandfather, wearing a
cloth cap over his bald head, waited beside Riley harnessed to the
buggy. The conductor helped my mother down the big step from
the train, as we descended into the era of small farms subsisting,

nations of independence one family small. I have written all this before; enough, except to acknowledge that on each trip I visited with my mother an embodied lost domain.

❖

WHEN JANE AND I left Michigan to settle here, in 1975, we entered and revivified the New Hampshire domain. Unpacking the boxes in 1997, I mostly recovered Connecticut. I exhumed mementos of Brock-Hall: milk bottles, ads cut from the *New Haven Register*, pencils with the dairy's "Pure-Pact" slogan. Other objects brought back other affections: an anthology of poems for children, *Silver Pennies*, from which my mother read to me; a stuffed toy dog my father brought me from a trip to New York, which I hugged to tatters. Remembered scenes flashed like film clips. I saw my father weeping (a father who weeps is a gift to his son, but it disturbed me then) over his misery working for a father who never wept. I recalled visiting Henry and Augusta's house on a Sunday when Henry Hall's saddle horse, slipping on ice, had rolled on him and broken his leg in three places. My Uncle Arthur sliced the boot off Henry's leg as Henry sat silent, teeth clenched, staring straight ahead without tears.

My grandfather was, they said, "a hard man." The Brock-Hall Dairy where my father labored was only a short distance from Winette Street, and he walked home for lunch. From an early age I was told that he shook his fist over my cradle, saying, "He's going to do what he wants to do." I grew up to reject my father's culture by following my father's advice, choosing a place and a work that were alien to him. My father stuck to the vow of the shaken

fist. A few days before he died, when *Time* praised my first book
of poems, a lead review with a photograph, he was ecstatic.

What did I do all day before I went to school? My mother read
aloud. I remember *Ping* and *Little Black Sambo*; I remember Va-
chel Lindsay's "The Moon's the North Wind's Cookie," from *Silver Pennies*. I listened to the radio, often with Aggie. I played with
neighborhood children or by myself in my room or in the back
yard. I overheard grown-ups talking. Sometimes on weekend
nights my parents invited other couples for drinks and bridge.
I lay in my bed hearing the teasing and laughing voices, which
grew louder as the evening progressed. Every word, every tone,
every laugh sounded purposeful, as if having fun were something
undertaken on purpose. But mostly the family evenings were silent, as my parents read books and magazines. I daydreamed. I
wondered what school would be like. In my fancy it was purple
and gold, luminous and untouchable. I imagined that one had to
be clean, one had to be good. I imagined that one was offered exquisite toys, like a small stagecoach, purple and gold with inlaid
jewels, too precious and too fragile to touch. My fantasy enriched
the schoolroom with dreadful grandeur—soaring, dark and aw-
ful as a cathedral. My imagination of school was identical to my
imagination of heaven.

The real kindergarten teacher, Miss Heatherington, was tall
and slim, kindly. For the first time I lived hour after hour among
other children. I was sweet on a girl named Marsha whose charm
was doing somersaults. One day the kindergarten class visited
the construction site of the new brick Brock-Hall Dairy building,
rising on Whitney Avenue just two blocks from the old wooden

structure. It was rare that anything got built in 1934. Brock-Hall erected its big new plant while the home-delivery milk business thrived despite the times. Milk was house-delivered because glass bottles were heavy to carry from the corner grocery. Families rich enough to own a car owned only one car, and the father drove it to work. Blocks of wooden houses woke to bottles lined up outside the screen door ready for the mother to make breakfast. Brock-Hall took pride in the cream line of its Grade A, which dove deeper than the cream lines of its competitors. Mothers poured off cream for coffee and cooking. On winter mornings, frozen cream pushed up the caps of bottles waiting on back porches.

The building was almost whole when we visited, and we toured its nascent offices, its laboratory that would test for butterfat content and bacteria, its main floor of pasteurizing machine and bottle washer that stretched out in aluminum glory, bright and big as an Airstream trailer. The bottle washer was stationed near the dairy's front windows, so that passersby could see it gleam as they drove down Whitney Avenue. At one end, men emptied crates of dirty milk bottles, stacking them upright in rows, which disappeared into the stomach of the great machine. After thumping and clatter—sometimes a bottle broke—the gleaming bottles, sparkling like ice or diamonds, appeared one by one on belts that carried them to machines dispensing Grade A or Grade B. Shining empty glass became sudden columns of white. Further machines capped the bottles and shuttled them toward wooden crates. At five or six in the morning, milkmen loaded their wagons and trucks with gray wooden crates of milk in quart bottles, and delivered Brock-Hall to the back steps. Meanwhile, raw milk from country farms entered in tall silvery cans at another portal for pasteurizing before bottling. Five years old, I was proud to be a Hall of Brock-Hall. For a while after the visit with my kindergarten mates, a small halo of celebrity hovered above me.

In other parts of the building, Brock-Hall made ice cream, cottage cheese, and butter. At the bottom of its acreage ran long stables for great-hoofed workhorses tended by old men who fed and groomed and shod them. Trucks worked only the faraway routes. As I grew up, the edifice and enterprise of Brock-Hall pulsed at the center of my Connecticut life. Ken Moseley, Johnny Murphy, Hal Schenk were my father's friends who worked at the dairy. My New Hampshire cousin Jim Walker, fired during the Depression from his job as manager of a Grant's store in Ohio, migrated to Hamden where my father found him work delivering milk. My early Connecticut contained no Yale University, although it was only four miles away; it contained no Winchester, the big arms manufacturer in New Haven. It contained grammar school and Brock-Hall. As I grew up, occasionally I worked at Brock-Hall for a few weeks in summer, to fill in when the office boy took his vacation. Mostly I delivered notes from employee to employee. I got to know Freddie Sauer in the supply room, and Agnes McKeon, who bossed the girls in the big office with its Burroughs adding machines and upright Royal typewriters. The managers or executives were familiar, like my father—who was treasurer, adding penciled numbers—and my Uncle Arthur, who occupied a series of superior positions. I knew some of the long-term milkmen, like my cousin Jim, who were later called Route Salesmen. When I was in my teens I helped deliver milk for ten days with the milkman Bo Mason, just recovering from surgery and unable to lift or carry. This chore came after the war, when fleets of trucks replaced the great horses, and Bo's route attended Connecticut's shoreline. We would park outside a house or cottage and Bo would tell me: "One A, one B, and a half pint of light cream. Don't leave the bottles where a screen door can knock them over."

Homogenization standardized the product in the 1950s. With a second car, people shopped at supermarkets that sold milk as a loss leader; half gallons in cartons gradually knocked out home delivery, and the dairy began struggling. Small local groceries that carried Brock-Hall milk died out. The dairy tried delivering other products, like eggs and orange juice. In drugstores, Brock-Hall ice cream flourished but did not provide income enough. The dairy still thrived in 1955 when my father died, and for a while income from its stock supported my mother. Then Brock-Hall merged with another company, which made things worse. The dairy stopped paying dividends before it closed down in the sixties. My mother took up substitute teaching, and the Brock-Hall plant that my kindergarten class had watched grow brick by brick turned derelict, trashed by vandals, until the wrecker's ball shattered it for new apartment buildings.

Toward the end of my first school year, we moved from Winette Street to Whitney Avenue, still a rented house but bigger and newer, on the corner of Harmon, back in Spring Glen a few blocks from the old Coram Street house. Spring Glen was more uniformly middle class than Whitneyville. Near us was a block of little stores: two drugstores, a liquor store, a one-man A & P, a dry goods store, a shoe repair shop. One drugstore sold Brock-Hall ice cream, and thus received my patronage when someone gave me a nickel. Wooden stools fronted a counter where Bill Bristol assembled milkshakes and sundaes and cones of vanilla, chocolate, or strawberry. Mr. Wallace tended the tiny A & P. He fetched and sold what was asked of him, using a long-handled clutch to reach a can of mincemeat or a roll of toilet paper stacked to the ceiling. Attached to the garage of our new house was a small workroom with a carpenter's bench, a vise, and a rack of tools. At the age of five I decided to become a carpenter. Moving day, my grandmother Augusta took me shopping in New Haven to keep me out of the way. She bought me tools; I remember an awl. I remember being careful to behave well with Augusta; I remember a lunch of chicken à la king in pastry shells. That summer, moving toward the age of six, I met the neighborhood boys. Some were children of Yale faculty. Because it was the 1930s, some spoke with accents, families that made early exits from Spain and Germany. Across the street George Buendia was one year older. My recollections of childhood play are mildly unpleasant: dripping noses, shouts, blows, arguments, skinned knees, shirts hanging out over knickers. Never until college did I feel comfortable in my own generation. From the house on Whitney Avenue, I retreated to the workroom where I pounded nails into the skin of wood.

In September I entered first grade. My teacher was Abbie Ford, who handled the slow track. When I was elevated to the higher level, my teacher was Abbie's sister Stephanie. Pupils were tracked carly, and, over the eight years we spent in Spring Glen Grammar School—a tenth of a long life—after first grade almost no one switched from one level to the other. Each year stretched out so far ahead, so great a proportion of the life; the identity of our single teacher was paramount. When I knew that in the next grade I would have an unpopular teacher, I lived in anguish looking ahead. (I could hope that she would get married. At that time, married women could not be teachers, which reveals a certain attitude toward sex.) Abbie and Stephanie Ford were stereotypical spinster grade-school teachers. Abbie was soft and white-haired and gentle. Stephanie was stiff, black-haired—it had to be dye—and strict. My spirit faltered when I entered her class, but it was under her instruction that I learned to read. For years I had looked forward to reading, which was what grown-ups did. I observed my parents every night, sitting in soft chairs, silently gazing into books and magazines. My father read *Time* and historical novels. He was a snob for well-made sentences, and would not read junk. He liked Hervey Allen and Kenneth Roberts. My mother read *Reader's Digest*, a bit of Frost and Thoreau (she had majored in English at Bates College, where my father majored in history), and more of Agatha Christie and Erle Stanley Gardner. When I became an arty adolescent, I deplored their literary taste; they should have been reading Proust and Hart Crane. Later I understood my good fortune in having parents who read books.

The first word I was taught to read, after weeks of memorizing the alphabet, was "that." Did my life begin with "that"? One's life begins on so many occasions, constructing itself out of accident derived from coincidence compounded by character. (Only the last is ordained, if it is ordained.) Though I learned to read in the first grade, I did not become a reader until the second, when I endured a long episode of whooping cough and spent four weeks at home in bed. The radio fed me fifteen-minute soap operas.

Ma Perkins became involved in Chinese tong wars. Mary Noble's missing husband wandered Asia, afflicted with amnesia. Belle helped out her impractical inventor husband Lorenzo Jones. I had brought home from school a big storybook, and when radio palled, I became a reader. I finished the book and my mother went to the library.

Despite books, the radio was a constant in my childhood. Every Sunday night my mother made a big platter of sandwiches which we ate in front of the Philco while we listened to Jack Benny. An hour later, Fred Allen came on. Daytime there were always the soap operas, and at night on weekdays there were epic productions starring Bob Hope and Bing Crosby. Sometimes I listened to them while I was in bed and supposed to be sleeping. I had a portable radio I kept under the cover, volume turned low. On weekends I listened to football in the autumn, with special avidity when Yale was a powerful team—Larry Kelly one year and Clint Frank the next; an Ivy League player actually won the Heisman Trophy. Spring, summer, and autumn we took rides in the car, a common form of entertainment in the thirties—inexpensive, with gas going at a dollar for five gallons, sometimes with a set of dishes thrown in—and on these rides we listened to baseball.

At school I fell in love with Miss Sudell, who taught the third grade. She invited Dottie Page and me to take the trolley into New Haven to choose prizes Miss Sudell gave out for excellence. After we made our choices, Miss Sudell bought us each a sundae. I suggested that our class seating be rearranged, so that Miss Sudell's desk stood in the middle of a U of children's desks, rather than facing the straight rows. I was overjoyed to come to class on Monday and find that Miss Sudell had done what I suggested.

Unpacking the boxes, I found a photograph from the *New Haven Register:* "Lucy W. Hall Elected President of Whitneyville Women's Club." Her face is thin and pretty, good cheekbones and chin. The photograph restores my young mother the comforter, before I lost her. (Losses make even stronger memories than transgressions. New Hampshire's cellar holes were models; a disappeared toy was as poignant as a vanished house.) Comforting me when I was sad or couldn't sleep, my mother crawled onto my bed, on top of the covers, and sang in my ear. Sometimes I made myself stay awake so that I could call out for her. She could not carry a tune, but tunes were not the point. The point was touch, and love, tenderness and adoration taken and given. I can feel her hand as she rubs my head, hear her soft thin voice in my ear singing the songs of her childhood: "Keep the Home Fires Burning"; "There's a Long, Long Trail A-Winding (into the Land of My Dreams)." I fell asleep at night on love's island, dozing in the warm arms of the sea. Love's island provides a standard that nothing in adulthood can quite live up to, something always sought, sometimes glimpsed in brief restoration, secured only by my wife Jane.

Against her will and her desire, Jane abandoned me in death, but my mother unwillingly abandoned me first. Beginning when I was six or seven, she withdrew into illness. When I came home from school she lay in her bed, sluggish, slow to respond. She had to push herself to do anything; on a Saturday afternoon she might take me by trolley into New Haven to watch an Abbott and Costello movie or a Shirley Temple. Gradually she lost the strength even to go to a movie. She became more and more vague and distant, unreachable, unreaching. I was desolate, expelled from paradise, and angry. It was my father who made me a school lunch while I ate breakfast, or on weekends treated me to breakfast at a diner. Of course he fretted over Lucy. Doctors came and went, prescribing rest and a bland diet. Her diet was already bland, even more skimpy than bland. Nothing tasted good; everything bothered her stomach. A stomach specialist arrived from New Haven, pronounced "nervous indigestion," and prescribed phenobarbital. Every week she became thinner. This woman who weighed 160 pounds in late middle age, 125 when she was young and healthy, dropped down to 68. She was vanishing. No one spoke of a psychiatrist. No one mentioned anorexia nervosa. Why would my mother slide into anorexia? Slimness was not then an American obsession. I think she was victim inside herself of the war of two landscapes and two cultures. Although she struggled to conform to Spring Glen, she was frequently reminded of her failures. When she conformed successfully, she betrayed New Hampshire and the farm.

When I was a child, there was only one bad thing about New Hampshire. The conflict between Connecticut and New Hampshire, in my mother's life and soul, generated a series of lies I was sworn not to reveal. In Connecticut, my mother drank, smoked, danced, wore makeup, and played cards. Her father Wesley was a fierce teetotaler—two brothers had taken to drink—but most prohibitions derived from my grandmother. Her church descended from Puritans and Calvinists who emigrated from England. The South Danbury Christian Church was plain, severe, without a cross or other idolatry. The minister wore black; vestments would be papist. When my mother was a girl, church was two hours Sunday morning and two more in the afternoon, sometimes with hymn singing at Christian Endeavor in the evening. On Sunday at the farm, animals were fed and cows milked, but there was no other work on the Sabbath. For entertainment, young people gathered on a weeknight to speak pieces, sing songs, drink coffee or soft cider, and debate a political topic: in 1898, "Resolved: That the United States Should Cease from Territorial Expansion." Drinking and smoking and card playing and dancing and swearing—"gosh" was unacceptable—were anathema. Absent from this catalogue of prohibition is sex. My father's Connecticut was shameful about sex, but the rural world took it for granted. It was natural: Animals did it, whereas cows and horses were not known to drink hard cider, play bridge, or puff on stogies. Sometimes a cousin's first child was born six months after the wedding; aside from a moment's *tsk-tsk*, there were no consequences. But let another cousin pass out in a tavern while playing poker, and disgrace was devastating. When my mother went to Bates College in the mill town of Lewiston, Maine, she had her first beer in the company of three young Catholic priests. She did not tell this story at home.

When she married and went to live in Connecticut, she seemed to accept her changed behavior as the normal way of the modern (speakeasy, flapper) world, but in her depths she must have felt moral turpitude. In her profound attachment to family, she needed to keep the worlds separate—and so she lied, she lied and lied. From earliest times I remember being reminded, as we neared New Hampshire by car or train, that I must never mention cigarettes or drinks or dancing or bridge. These reminders were urgencies; it was insistent, this necessity to conspire and protect my mother by the lie of withholding. When her mother

Kate died at ninety-seven, Lucy at seventy-two was still conceal-
ing her debauched suburban habits.

❖

A RECOVERED ANOREXIC once told me, "And then I decided to
live." After two years of her skeletal distance, my mother gained a
little weight. A new doctor told her to get out of bed, go out to dinner, have a drink, enjoy yourself. She decided to live, and gradually, over a few years of intermittent vagueness or inattention,
she did. She became caring again, she was tender, but her earlier
withdrawal from the years of singing in my ear left me imprinted
with loss. Much of my poetry has been elegiac, even morbid, beginning with laments over New Hampshire farms and extending
to the death of my wife. "After the first death there is no other."

In 1936 my parents bought a six-room house, still in Spring
Glen, on the corner of Ardmore and Greenway, in a neighborhood of six-room houses. They bought it from a bank, after a
foreclosure. They found it gratifying to own their own house,
more modest than the Whitney Avenue place but their own, although my father from time to time spoke with sadness about
the unknown family that had suffered foreclosure. We moved
in; we took possession of a small, dark, well-constructed, mock-
Tudor house on a small street-corner lot. My parents were thirty-
three when they bought the house. My father died there nineteen years later, and it was in this house that my mother turned
ninety—looking out the window at birds and schoolchildren
and busy traffic. There were few cars in 1936 on Ardmore and
Greenway; I walked to Spring Glen school a mile away.

The bus to New Haven stopped only one long block up Ardmore. I had a room to myself, next to my parents' bedroom. When we moved in, a horse and wagon still delivered ice to families with an icebox and no refrigerator. Our house had the usual coal furnace. Men with coal-stained faces treaded on each other's heels as they carried sacks of black anthracite on their backs and rumbled it down the chute into the coal bin. I watched my father emptying ash and shoveling flammable black stone into the orange fire as I stood beside him, compelled to gaze into the fury. A few years later my parents afforded a trim blue steel gas furnace, fuel piped from underground. When he had scrubbed coal dust off the whitewash of the cellar walls, my father bought a ping-pong table. Outside, I walked in a neighborhood scrap of woods around Johnson's Pond, bordered by houses now. Boys played hockey there all winter. Not me. I tried but failed to skate. In warm weather it was a place of adventure and fear. I caught turtles and brought them home where they died. Sometimes I hid under bushes around Johnson's Pond to evade assault in the wars of boyhood. On a vacant lot nearby, the neighborhood played baseball. Captains chose sides, fisting up a bat, top fist getting first pick. In memory, I am always chosen last.

Saturdays, my father worked the old half day and came home in the afternoon to rest or rake leaves or clean gutters or mow the lawn or chop ice from the sidewalk. Sunday afternoons we took rides in the Studebaker, never the same route twice. I was thrilled by my father's geographic skill; he remembered the roads from long summers spent delivering milk when he was young. In the fall we drove through Hamden's countryside, sometimes stopping at a stand for cider or root vegetables. We drove along the coastline in cold weather past boarded-up hot dog stands and cottages, gazing from the heated car into the frigid waves of Long Island Sound. I sat in the back seat watching my father's neatly shaved neck under his fedora. I gazed at my mother's earrings as they swayed under the hat she set on her head whenever she left the house. We ended each ride at Al Holcome's drugstore, eating sundaes of Brock-Hall ice cream as we sat in wire chairs at little marble-topped tables. Each week, we approached Al's from a new direction.

When I was nine, my Aunt Jenny died of cancer. My grandmother Hall's sister, she and her husband Willard owned a cottage on Long Island Sound, which we had often visited on summer weekend afternoons. Jenny died quickly, and at her funeral her brother George, who owned the Studebaker dealership that supplied the family cars, felt a sudden sharp pain in his back. He died of cancer two months later. I lay in bed after George's funeral, repeating a sentence over and over in my head: "Death has become a reality." It was as if I were phrasing an item to repeat in a memoir. I dramatized myself, and took every opportunity to write myself new roles. I must have been ten or so when I woke one night to hear my parents quarreling. They never quarreled in front of me. I heard sounds or tones that I had never heard before, not from them nor from other grown-ups. The next night I stayed awake on purpose, and heard them again be cruel to each other. Night after night I lay awake to listen, fascinated and appalled. In the morning I looked at them for signs of the rage I had heard in the middle of the night, but they were the same quiet, mild people I had always known. Everything appeared to be the same. I went to school wearing long socks and corduroy knickers, like all the other boys. I took pleasure in hypocrisy as by day

I played the role of Donnie, only son of Lucy from New Hampshire who washed and ironed and cooked meals, only son of Don who worked at the dairy and came home at five-thirty every night tired and humiliated.

The usual threesome by daylight, we entered an underside by night. Duplicity, and my concurrence in duplicity, fed my appetite for the wicked and the extraordinary. I became aware that my father loved another woman, and the woman was Aggie our maid—earlier I had wept when my mother told me that Aggie would work for us no longer—whom I had loved when I was little. My father's adultery was commonplace, I know by now, and it had, besides lust, its commonplace excuses. With her illness, my mother had detached from my father as she had detached from me. When she felt better she and I often visited New Hampshire. Alone in an empty house, my father sought comfort. This betrayal was my father's attempt to alter the circumstances of his sadness. It succeeded in one particular. When the crisis had ended, affair over, my strong mother prevailed and took more care of my weak father, and gave up going home so frequently to New Hampshire. Eventually, they behaved again with an affection that I believe was genuine, love constructed of my mother's powerful solicitude and my father's grateful if guilty submission.

❖

WHEN THE WEATHER was good, my father and I played catch outdoors, football in autumn, baseball in spring and summer. He had his old glove from the years when he played semipro shortstop. As early as possible I determined to be a pitcher—as later I determined to be John Keats and T. S. Eliot. My father bought a catcher's mitt and squatted on the Greenway Street sidewalk: "Put 'er there." I put her there, sometimes, but frequently hurled wild pitches that flew ten feet over his head and rolled down the suburban gutter. I knew that my wildness left him impatient, as he loped and trotted to retrieve the scuffed leather. Sometimes I threw over his head twice in a row, and headed back to the screen door in shame.

At ping-pong, I did better. Until I was eleven or twelve, my father always won, but I scored points against him. He was in his late thirties when he started shaking. I began to beat him, at first two out of three, then every game. I teased him to play, when he felt too tired to play. After supper when he smoked Chesterfields and picked up his book, I swung my hand back and forth, clicking my fingers. Reluctantly he arose and we descended the cellar stairs for our three games. Now and then I cajoled my mother to watch. For years she was still sometimes vague, which irritated me. Once an errant ball bounced past her where she sat, and my father called "Luce!" but she did not react. He trotted across the cellar to retrieve the ball. "She didn't hear you," I said. "She'll hear you in about two years." After another rally she reacted. "I didn't like that crack," she said.

Though usually my father sat in the evening smoking and reading a historical novel, sometimes he brought work home from the office. He sat at the desk in the sunroom adding columns of figures, neatly writing sums with a soft pencil. He had grown up bad at arithmetic, but through his work (always antithetical to his ability and character) he became quick and accurate in simple addition. It was his pride that he could add columns of figures in his head more rapidly than someone sitting beside him who tapped at an adding machine. Often he came home from the office shaking, pale, and weepy. Maybe someone had discovered him in a business mistake. Or a milkman was found embezzling money, and got himself fired, and my father felt betrayed and angry; even more, he felt sorrowful over the milkman's family, no money and Christmas coming. Sometimes he wept because a colleague at the office had been sarcastic, maybe his younger brother Art, who took to business with gusto over competition and joy in making money. When my father wept he was ashamed because men did not weep; he rushed out of the room to hide himself. It was hard to see him so sorrowful, but I knew I was not to notice or respond.

My Uncle Arthur bought an island, southernmost of the Thimbles, in Long Island Sound off Guilford. It was near shore, and a short bridge connected it to the mainland. We went there for picnics, for swimming, and for rides on Art's Chris-Craft. There were parties at the cabana they put up across island from their huge old timber house, built to withstand a hurricane, that withstood the hurricane of 1938. We drove there often, a pleasure modified by its testament to the greater prosperity and shrewdness of the younger brother.

There were other, more independent pleasures. Rarely, we took an exciting Saturday excursion to Savin Rock, an old-fashioned amusement park by Long Island Sound, rides and cotton candy stands. Jimmies hot dogs were split and fried and served flat on a hamburger roll with a delirium of condiments. I loved the rides: an antique roller coaster, bump-'em cars, a tunnel of love that featured a long swoop into water after the moments of romantic darkness, a haunted house. My father threw a baseball and knocked over furry animal dolls and wooden milk bottles for prizes. (It was still the Depression; if you were skillful, you might win five pounds of sugar.) My father enjoyed the games, and I had glimpses of a happier man, and heard stories of happier times, when he had played baseball as a boy and enjoyed a boy's adventures. He told exciting stories about fighting fires when he was in his teens and a member of the Whitneyville Volunteer Fire Department; he climbed up on a freight car to hose down a burning warehouse.

To Ardmore Street every spring came a catalogue of mail-order fireworks from a distributor in Indiana. I spent hours reading descriptions of firecrackers, pinwheels, and rockets, with special attention to nightworks. I made check marks next to dozens of items, and one Saturday afternoon my father and I made out the order. In a few weeks a great long box arrived in the mail, long because of the length of rockets. Unpacking that box, I set out on the living room floor rows of fireworks according to category—green fire here, squiggly fire-worms there, cheap small Chinese firecrackers in a pile beside big thick heavy superbombs. Punk was free. I packed and unpacked the box, in meditation and expectation, until the glorious Fourth of July. Our town and New Haven had banned fireworks after a kid threw a lighted firecracker into a fireworks stand, blowing it up and killing the woman who presided over it, but there were little country towns that had no such laws. In the morning we drove into the country armed with our daytime munitions and parked on a dirt road, lit our punk, and banged a hundred bangs. My sad father grinned with pleasure; I was ecstatic, and the best part came at night. We drove to my uncle's island and set off nightworks, burning and blasting and painting the ocean air with rockets that bloomed into orange chrysanthemums or dangled bunches of purple grapes, and then exploded to shatter the air. It was a happier day than Christmas.

As my father grew older, and Brock-Hall no longer required the Saturday half day at the office, his Saturday mornings became eighteen holes of golf. He looked forward all week to his driving and chipping and putting, to the comradeship of his foursome. Sometimes now we took rides in the Studebaker both Saturday and Sunday afternoons, and from April through September listened to the gentle intimate drawl of Red Barber as he broadcast the games of the Brooklyn Dodgers. My father's love of the game went far back—my mother took me in a basket to his semipro games—but it was Red Barber who brought my mother and me into baseball, and we followed the fortunes of the Dodgers from the cellar to the pennant to repetitive losses to the Yankees in the World Series. Occasionally we drove to Ebbets Field on a weekend afternoon to watch the Dodgers. In 1941, at Yankee Stadium, I saw the first game of the World Series; the Yankees won on a Joe Gordon home run in the ninth inning. In the autumn of 1955, my terminal father watched on an eight-inch TV screen as for the first time the Dodgers beat the Yankees and won the World Series.

When I walked home from the seventh grade, and the eighth, I was often alone in the Ardmore Street house, as my mother, gaining weight and strength, returned to shopping and bridge and the ceremonial activities of the American Association of University Women. In the cellar, I propped half the ping-pong table upright, wedged against the ceiling, and volleyed for hours by myself. I liked sitting alone in the dark living room with my sheepdog Zippy, as I played over and over again the ten-inch 78 of Connee Boswell singing "The Kerry Dance," remembering that she sat in a wheelchair as she sang about dancers. I loved solitude, an only child who did not care for other children. I threw a toy bone in the air for Zippy to catch, sometimes snatching it out of the air just before it entered his range. Unpacking the boxes in 1998, I found the toy bone, and when I smelled it saw Zippy again and heard Connee Boswell's voice.

In seventh grade we had different teachers according to subject, filing from English to social studies to arithmetic to general science. Every other week we had art and music, at each of which I was helpless. Reading was always there, after the fortunate whooping cough. I started to read grown-up books, using the library of the Spring Glen Grammar School. I remember how the librarian Mrs. Goldberg suggested that maybe *Madame Bovary* was a little *old* for me at twelve — which made it not only attractive but urgent. I read *Anna Karenina* that year also, specializing in adultery. I read everything, and I don't believe I noticed the difference between Henry Fielding and Ellery Queen. I kept a record of what I read, not for anyone else's eyes, but with a greed of acquisition. I happened upon a list years later, where I said that *Portrait of a Lady* was "wonderful, terrific" and *Mr. Moto Changes Trains* was "terrific, wonderful."

On the playground of Spring Glen Grammar School, certain male bodies became noticeably strong and agile, the athletes who would thrive at the center of adolescent society. These boys skated on Johnson's Pond and improvised hockey games. Certain girls developed breasts and turned pretty. Boys stopped wearing knickers and turned to long pants. I was no good in any sport, cut from the eighth-grade baseball team. At the same time, I found myself more and more drawn to girls. When I read *Madame Bovary* and *Anna Karenina*, my understanding of what took place in locked carriages was imperfect, but I knew that it was something wicked and worth dying for. Sexual talk among the boys was commonplace and inaccurate. I heard about the bloody rag. In general science we studied adhesion, the force that attracts bodies to each other, which was good for snickers on the playground. Then there was capillary attraction, the force that draws liquids up small passages. Something called "nocturnal emission" occurred while I slept, but these orgasms did not lead me to assist myself. Every morning I had an erection, which I enjoyed, but was embarrassed to come down to breakfast because my pants stuck out. Sitting in the bathroom I learned that I could make it go away if I hummed a popular song of the day, "Elmer's Tune." I did not masturbate, because I imbibed my father's intense anxiety about masturbation. It was not merely a prohibition but a shattering guilt that consumed him, with which he infected me. Neither of my parents ever spoke to me about sex. My mother at last decided to do something about it, and from the public library brought home a book that purported to tell a child "the facts of life." How revealing the old phrase is; by its airy abstraction it avoids any erotic suggestion while it claims—*The, Facts, Of, Life*—as much eminence for eros as Freud did. It's my recollection that by the time I read the book, I knew what it would tell me. I sat solemn and straight-faced, aware that my mother stole glances at me. I was still reading when my father came home from the office. My mother spoke to him at the door, and he paced up and down, watching, smoking Chesterfields, abruptly grinding one out and lighting another. When I finished the book he asked me if it was one of those books that said it was all right to play with yourself. It wasn't, and warnings against self-abuse were frequent. The Boy Scout Handbook condemned the practice under the topic of conservation. My father was more extreme than the commonplace. When I was twelve or thirteen, he drove me to the Whitneyville Country Club, where a caddie in his twenties, brain damaged, drooled and spasmed and twitched his hand against his fly. My father told me that playing with himself had made the caddie a moron. I did not argue, but I knew it was not true. I felt superior to him because he tried to influence me by telling me something absurd.

Gaudeamus Igitur

WHEN I WAS TWELVE, I was girl-crazy and crazy for horror movies like *Frankenstein* and *The Wolf Man.* I doted on a kind, friendly girl in the seventh grade. I went to her house on a summer afternoon and we played catch. Another girl lived a block away from me. We lay chastely on her bed—fully clothed, discreetly separated—when her mother peeked in, her face rank with anxiety. In eighth grade I went loony over a tall blonde from the slow track whom I had known all through Spring Glen Grammar School. She was beautiful and I was lovesick. She would not let me kiss her. I took her to the high school prom when we were freshmen, and we had our picture taken. I remember the photograph, her flowered skirt and black velvet top against which she spread out her long yellow hair—Susan Frisbee. I remember all their names.

Lon Chaney, Jr., played the title role in *The Wolf Man* and its sequels. There was always a moment when the mild-mannered citizen grew thick hair on his face while his eyeteeth elongated and he became the werewolf, scourge of mist-shrouded woods and doubtless of tall pretty girls with blond hair. Vampires and werewolves were ordinary folk who became alienated powerful outsiders, pure evil, therefore romantic, attractive, and dangerous. I told a neighbor boy, two years older, how I took the bus into New Haven alone on a Saturday afternoon to see horror films. He told me that if I liked that sort of thing, I ought to read Edgar Allan Poe. I didn't know this author's name, but in my parents' bookshelves I found a boxed two-volume set of his works, one of those cheap fancy editions that the Book-of-the-Month Club called Dividends. I was dumbstruck. It was the *best stuff* I had read in my entire life!

Elevated by terror and necrophilia, I read Poe's tales and poems — all the dead young women, some of whom walked at night albeit dead. I wanted to write stories like these stories, poems like these poems. I wanted to *be* Edgar Allan Poe, and I wrote my first poem, "The End of All," which was morbid but with none of Poe's sound. Every time I say it, or write it down, it's a little different.

> Have you ever thought
> Of the nearness of death to you?
> It follows you through the day,
> It screams through the night
> Until that moment when,
> In monotones loud,
> Death calls your name.
> Then, then comes the end of all.

Friends tell me it's the best thing I've done. I never showed it to my parents. Probably I showed it to girls. I tried writing morbid stories as well, but did not finish them. In my parents' wall of books I found *Israfel,* a biography of Poe written by Hervey Allen, and read it through, discovering that Poe was already reading Keats and Shelley when he was fourteen years old. I had not heard of Keats and Shelley, but required myself to be two years smarter than Poe. I saved up my allowance and bought the Modern Library Giant *Keats and Shelley* ($1.25). I still have it. I wrote further poems, in a diction that resembled the early nineteenth century. Every afternoon, I shut the door of my bedroom to write: Poetry was secret, dangerous, wicked, and delicious.

In general the arts—theater and music and painting and sculpture and poetry—carry with them an aura of sexual freedom and license, some arts and artists more than others: jazz and rock musicians, dancers, actresses. Typically, readers have felt something erotic in poetry, something adventurous, wayward, sensuous, and forbidden. Late romanticism created the *poète maudit:* outlaw, madman, bohemian, overthrower of social convention—considerably alien to Ardmore Street. But even before artist decadents drank absinthe in dark cafés, poetry was sensual by its nature—in its internal structure, in its bodiliness, especially in its carnality of sound. Poetry is more erotic than fiction, which is why female poets were so rare until the mid-twentieth century. Jane Austen and George Eliot were permitted to write great novels, but the only great nineteenth-century woman poet was the eccentric eremite Emily Dickinson. In the first half of the twentieth century, Marianne Moore was equally exceptional. The vast increase in the number of good women poets has coincided with sexual liberation.

My environment when I was thirteen was largely horror movies, girls, and poetry, but other things were happening. On December 7, 1941, I was listening as Red Barber broadcast a professional football game between the New York Giants and the Brooklyn Dodgers (he called Brooklyn games in two sports) while my parents napped upstairs. Barber interrupted the play-by-play to announce that Japanese airplanes had bombed Pearl Harbor. I knew that my parents would have the radio on low, and I called up the stairs, "Did you hear that?" My father called down; they had. My father, at thirty-eight (his birthday was the day before), expected to be drafted. From that moment until 1945, war was the weather everyone walked in. All radio broadcasts reported on the war; entertainers visited the troops; cigarette companies sent free cartons overseas when a baseball player hit a home run. We were citizens of the war effort; we collected scrap; meat, sugar, and gasoline were rationed. Schools became obsessed with fitness. Sixteen-year-old boys took war jobs in factories after school. In the newspaper I read every day about offensives, defeats, and atrocities; I heard about invasions of Pacific islands and massive bombings in Europe. It seemed impossible that newspapers would have anything to talk about after the war. Like everyone male, I knew that at eighteen I would wear a uniform and fight.

My father would not, because of his age, but we did not yet know it. The notion of being drafted made him nervous; and it made him nervous to be a male not in uniform. I remember a drunk, about to be drafted, who accosted him, accusing him of staying out of the military while conspiring to induct others. For a while my parents drove regularly to the Waverly Inn, saving up their gas coupons, to drink and eat dinner twice a week. Eating out and drinking, as the doctor suggested, contributed to my mother's recovery. Twice a week they drank multiple Black & White Scotch and sodas, sitting in a booth among other regulars in the bar, which was largely empty. Jimmy Heflin the bartender sat with us often, his face under his red hair turning redder and redder as he tanked up. The sloshed grown-ups had little to say to me. I loved it that I was alien; it was more agreeable to be alien among grown-ups than among schoolmates. Now and then my father would change a dollar into twenty nickels and send me to the pinball machine. I daydreamed endlessly in my virtual solitude, thinking of poetry. Our waiter was George Savakas, joshing and servile, who brought me Cokes while I played. Now and then my mother would go to the ladies' room and put her finger down her throat—to clear her head, she explained. My father drove home carefully. After a while—maybe a year—these excursions into alcohol slowed down, then stopped.

In June of 1942 Spring Glen Grammar School graduated its eighth grade, and as class president I made the graduation speech—which my father wrote. I knew what I wanted for a graduation present: *The Harvard Classics*. Book supplements still advertised this set of fifty volumes—Homer, Shakespeare, Adam Smith, Charles Darwin, Dante—edited in 1909 by former president Charles W. Eliot of Harvard; great books before Great Books. My parents found a used set, handsome and thickly bound in green cloth, for twenty-five dollars. I was determined to read it all. I never did, but from time to time I still read or reread an old volume from a shelf upstairs, the books transported in the boxes from Ardmore Street.

From school and Connecticut, every summer as I grew older, I rode the train alone north to my grandparents in New Hampshire, where I fed and watered the chickens, and hayed with my grandfather, until school started after Labor Day. My parents visited for a week in August. My Aunt Nan and Uncle Dick dropped by from Tilton, and Dick and I played badminton, until he joined the merchant marine and was stationed in Boston. My Aunt Caroline—the aunt I was closest to—spent time at the farm while her husband Everett, who had been in the Navy in the First War, sailed on cargo ships carrying goods to Europe in convoy, evading German U-boats. I loved Caroline, who had spent a summer at the Winette Street house when I was little, as she attended Yale summer school, and accomplished my toilet training. She was my literary aunt, who had told me stories then about a Greek wanderer who tricked a one-eyed giant when the giant wanted to eat him. In Connecticut, she dated a friend of my parents, who asked her to marry him, but she turned him down. She had many boyfriends and did not marry until she was almost forty. When her younger sister Nan married Dick, Caroline decided to accept the next man who proposed, and thus acquired my Uncle Everett. She visited the farm when Everett was away, and we went swimming together, we took walks, and she crawled into my bed early each morning to cuddle. One morning when I was twelve, or maybe thirteen, Caroline suddenly leapt out of bed and said that we couldn't cuddle anymore, that I was getting too grown-up. At the time, I didn't understand.

As a freshman at Hamden High School—a thousand pupils!—I began to know students who did not resemble the people I had known in grammar school. Spring Glen was the most middle class of the districts that fed Hamden High, and for the first time I came to know the sons and daughters of recent immigrants. In the hallways I heard southern Italian sounds; "pizza" was pronounced "ah-*beats.*" I heard boys saluting each other, "Eh, paisan!" I hung out with children of the working class and made other forays outside Spring Glen. Sometimes on Friday nights

I went to a Boy Scout meeting a few miles away at a New Haven church. I was a desultory Scout—never more than a Tender-foot—and attended meetings only to get out of the house, but going to Boy Scouts altered my life. One night as we gathered I chatted with a sophisticated sixteen-year-old Scout, and we boasted to each other. I bragged that I had written a poem in study hall that day. "Do you write *poems?*" he said. "Yes. Do you?" He hesitated a moment, out of drama, not shyness. "It is my profession." I had never heard anyone speak so thrilling a sentence. (In the movie *Bonnie and Clyde,* Clyde Barrow says, "We rob banks.") Dave Potter explained that he had dropped out of school in order to devote his time to writing poems. I was dazzled, and instantly ascended into hero worship. Dave knew Yale undergraduates who studied poetry and even wrote it. Thus, at fourteen I sat in a Yale dormitory room, permitted to hear discussions of modern poetry. With my allowance, I bought a hardcover *Collected Poems* of T. S. Eliot, for $2.50. I annotated it throughout, consistent in misspelling. Beside "I show you fear in a handful of dust," I wrote "eppigrammatic simbolism." (I have the book.) Beside Ezra Pound's name in the dedication to "The Waste Land," I wrote "nertz"—an emphatic negative of the moment, used by comedians and schoolchildren. I understood that Pound broadcast for Mussolini. From my new literary acquaintance, I heard about a great modern poet who lived forty miles north in Hartford. Disconcertingly, he worked in the insurance business.

Among Yale college freshmen, I could almost pass. I looked old for my age. It was convenient to look older if one was to be a romantic desperate figure. Alone in New Haven one night after a movie I walked to a bar that was known to be wicked, where sailors picked up girls. I bought a beer and practiced looking twenty-one. An attractive young woman in a blue dress asked me for a nickel so that she could play the jukebox. I panicked; I shook; I mumbled. I *knew* I should be bold with her. I gave her a nickel and, with my heart pounding, bolted from the bar and took a bus back to Hamden, to the safety of my bedroom beside my parents'. (I wrote a poem called "Night Wanderer.") At high school I went to football games and fell in love with cheerleaders, especially a small blonde with pretty legs and a tall brunette with breasts. I followed them in the corridors unable to speak to them. I did not show them my poems, but I must have bragged of my ambition; athletes addressed me, casually, as "fruit poet." I wanted everyone to know that I was a poet, though "fruit poet" was not what I had in mind. Poetry was a figure I cut.

It was not only a figure I cut. I loved *poems,* reading them for hours, saying them aloud, trying to write them. When I finished drafting a poem, I went back to the start and revised it. I worked hard to write poems—and equally hard to establish myself as fascinating, or at least weird. When I was talking with a girl, or with a boy who could be trusted to spread the word, I spoke a particular sentence from time to time, without providing a reason for delivering the information. I would announce, "Dead people don't like olives," and ten minutes later say again, "Dead people don't like olives."

Dave Potter lived a bus ride away, down Whitney Avenue, and we saw each other at least once a week, at his house or mine or in a Yale room occupied by an aged freshman. Decades later, my mother told me that she and my father worried about this association, that "something might be going on." I don't believe I even knew about homosexuality, the lid was so tight. Dave's parents were old and content to let him go his own way. Maybe they were afraid of him, with his dry and sarcastic manner. Dave was a poet first and a socialist second, and I inhaled his romantic politics. Being a socialist required Dave to be nasty about businessmen, which I found convenient in my need to feel superior to my family. But my passion was not for politics. Poetry was my passion, and it was my chosen means of eminence or notoriety.

But at fourteen almost anything would do. In 1943 the American Legion, composed of First World War veterans, funded an oratorical contest for high school students on the subject "The Challenge of the War to American Youth." My patriotic paean under that title carried no hint of subversive or socialist ideas, nor did it reveal that dead people didn't like olives. Winning, I accepted tribute from sources that I thought to despise, and my hypocrisy only completed my satisfaction, because I was deceiving *them*. I won the high school contest and the area contest. I was scheduled to compete in the statewide finals at Hartford, but on the great day woke up with measles. I believe I would have won. Other contestants revealed that our government was composed of executive, legislative, and judicial branches, or expressed praise for the Bill of Rights, or assailed the moral philosophy of Adolf Hitler. My success was founded not on thought or fact but on rhetoric. Originally I wrote the speech in lines of free verse, which no one listening suspected. I had been reading Carl Sandburg and the *Saturday Evening Post* war poems of Joseph Auslander. The lines made a noise like old-fashioned political oratory—Walt Whitman was distantly and dimly behind them, through Sandburg—and when the speech was published it collapsed easily into paragraphs.

> There have been other wars before this—hundreds, thousands, millions, man against man, nation against nation, continent against continent, thought against thought, theory against theory, supposition against supposition.
>
> Might and right have spilled their Blood in their eternal conflict before . . .

I dismissed charges that American youth were "leftwingist." I compared Germany to Sparta and spoke of "the gaunt twins—war and death." Add to bombast and rhetoric a booming voice and dramatic rhythmic pauses. I overwhelmed the judges, and measles did not end the fame of my speech. I was asked to deliver it to other American Legion posts, where I received standing ovations. I was asked to repeat it at the dedication of Hamden's Honor Roll, a scroll naming Hamden servicemen, some of them killed. I spoke outdoors, on a windy day, to two thousand people, and was told that no one missed a word. After the speech I was approached by a middle-aged man who identified himself as printer for the Yale University Press. He asked to do the speech as a pamphlet, and thus I went public with my first work. A bibliography refers to it as *"The Challenge of the War to American Youth: An Address by Donald A. Hall, Jr., Freshman, Hamden High School.* [n.l.: n.p.], 1943 . . ."

My oratory, and my big voice, related to another ambition. For a while, in pursuit of fame, I considered that I might be an actor as well as a poet. In freshman year I played the lead in the senior play, a hoary Broadway item called *The Charm School.* Miss Miniter cast it in the autumn and we rehearsed all year for one performance in the spring. Miss Miniter asked my opinion about casting the female lead, whom I would kiss in the play. I suggested a beautiful, untalented candidate who was reputed to be the fastest girl in Hamden High. (She dated Yale students.) The teacher demurred, but to my pleasure cast the second-fastest girl in Hamden High. I enjoyed my hour on the stage, and kissing the second-fastest girl—only in public—but poetry gradually won out over acting. I kept finding poems to love and imitate. In freshman English we used a literature text by Louis Untermeyer that included H.D. (Hilda Doolittle), who wrote imagist poems. She was a useful model for a fourteen-year-old, with her concentration on the particular physical image and on a Greeky sound emphasizing long vowels or diphthongs. Under her influence, I wrote "Wind-in-Storm," which came out in the annual Hamden High literary magazine, *The Cupola,* and was judged best poem.

Sophomore year, Miss Miniter wanted me to take the young lead in *Our Town,* but I decided to concentrate on poems. I refused, she insisted, I was stubborn; I took the small role of the drunken choirmaster, which required little rehearsal, and every afternoon I walked home from Hamden High School, greeted my mother, climbed to my room, closed my door, and wrote poetry. I wrote the verse play *The Folly of Existence,* and poems about haying with a grandfather on a New Hampshire farm. Halfway through rehearsals of *Our Town,* our drama teacher and director took the cast into Manhattan to see a professional production of the play. I remember two moments. At some point I detached myself from the group—poor Miss Miniter, escorting a dozen teenagers through the streets of New York—and entered the bar of the Hotel Edison. I ordered a Scotch and soda, my parents' drink, and was served. At another point I detached myself from the horde and took a companion with me, Jo Anne, who played Emily, the female lead in *Our Town*. During rehearsals we had looked at each other; in New York we looked at each other again: The city was aphrodisiac. I took her by the hand and we lost the rest of our party. We stepped inside the foyer of an apartment building and kissed desperately, mouths open, tongues licking tongues. I had necked in a balcony, but I had never kissed like this, nor pressed my body into a girl's as she leaned back against a wall. When our faces detached I remember how she looked—lipstick gone, face slathered, eyes wide in a panic of desire. Twenty-five years before the sexual revolution, our adventure went no further. We staggered out to recover an anxious Miss Miniter.

Back home, Jo Anne and I dated. Walking up the school stairs she twisted her body backward to gaze at me, a gesture I recognized as theatrical. I remember rolling with her on the carpet of her living room, her dress riding up. Before she and her family took a two-week holiday to Florida, I asked her to the prom my sophomore year. Then I performed my first betrayal. While Jo Anne was away, I asked another girl to the prom. Julie was pretty, sexy, shuffling through high school corridors with books clasped to her bosom and pelvis thrust forward. She was the daughter of a single mother who cooked for rich people, and after a date we sat kissing in a small servant's living room. With my arm around her I felt for the first time the swell of a breast; even if it was only the *side* of a breast, the softness was paradisal. My heart beat wildly for her prettiness, for the sexiness of her posture and manner.

(I wrote her a poem, and I believe she had the spunk to laugh out loud: In its amative ecstasy, my poem kissed the universe, causing something like a drizzle.) When Jo Anne returned from Florida she no longer had a date for the prom. I remember how forlorn she looked; I remember her studying to pretend that it didn't matter.

Every now and then I sent poems to magazines. Printed rejection slips arrived regularly from the *Atlantic, The New Yorker. The Nation* returned my poems with a note beginning, "If you really are fourteen . . ." My mother admired and praised my tenacity. I sent out short stories also. It was poetry that I loved most—but I wanted as well to be a *writer.* In sophomore year I began publishing regularly in another forum. New Haven had two newspapers, both unreadable, the morning *Journal-Courier* and the afternoon *New Haven Register.* They hired high school boys to cover high school sports, and Hamden High's previous stringer passed the job to me. The *Register* rewarded me with ten cents a column inch. The *Journal-Courier* paid me in bylines, "Don A. Hall," and every now and then a sports editor called Scotty MacDonald slipped me two bucks. As a reporter I rode on team buses and sat with cheerleaders, for whom I was a harmless mascot. Often I came home late from a Friday night basketball game and telephoned the paper a brief story with statistics. Hockey was the glamorous sport in high school Hamden. Saturday nights there were doubleheaders in the New Haven Arena, four high schools, and I would write up both games for the morning *Sunday Register.* The games ended late, shortly before deadline, and I sat in the sports department typing with one finger while the sports editor lurked over me. When I had finished a paragraph he would rip it out of the typewriter and dispatch it to compositors. He wore a green eyeshade.

At Hamden High, I continued to detach myself from the people I had grown up with. Jo Anne was from Spring Glen, Julie not. I made friends who came from the State Street district. One was the son of a Calabrian who had charge of the gardens in East Rock Park. My closest friend's parents were from Poland, his father a short-order cook, and another's people had fled Bela Kuhn in Hungary. With these friends, who were less conventional than my Spring Glen classmates, I could be a poet without ridicule. My State Street gang formed what we called a fraternity, invented a ceremony, and initiated ourselves. Of meetings I remember little except that we read aloud the dirty parts of *Studs Lonigan* and sometimes had a party, which meant that we got drunk. At the end of sophomore year, when I left Hamden High for boarding school, the frat gave me a going-away party and a present. As I departed for the great world, by way of a cold-hearted all-male school in a New Hampshire village, my fraternity brothers gave me a condom.

I left my State Street friends for Phillips Exeter Academy, in 1944 a compound of seven hundred suburban Republican boys taught by elderly conservatives. I went there because of my parents' ambitions for me, especially my father's. He had attended high school in New Haven, before Hamden had one, and took mechanical drawing for which he had no aptitude. His parents knew nothing of education and had pushed him toward mechanical drawing on the recommendation of friends who said it was useful for a boy. As he was about to graduate from Hillhouse, other friends of his parents counseled college; the Hall Dairy was thriving, and by 1920 prosperous parents sent their kids to college. But for college you needed Latin, not required for mechanical drawing. After his graduation, my father spent one year at Cushing Academy in Ashburnham, Massachusetts. It was the best thing his parents ever did for him. He had been depressed through high school, graduating as the second-shortest male in a class of a thousand; at Cushing he grew three inches. He took Greek instead of Latin, excelled at history and English, and sprinted on the track team. Although his social life was restricted—the school advised parents that students needed no pocket money; he stayed in his room while classmates bought nickel sodas—he thrived, he excelled. Separated from his parents, he was happy. The headmaster, who befriended him, recommended Bates College, where he met my mother, who had taken four years of Latin at high school in the mill town of Franklin, New Hampshire.

They were an unlikely pair—Connecticut suburb and New Hampshire farm, the cultures more different then than now. (An Amish girl dates a boy from Little Italy.) They fell in love, and when they graduated wanted to marry, but in 1925 a couple did not marry without enough to live on. Lucy took a job as a high school teacher in New Hampshire for a thousand dollars a year. Don could have returned to the dairy for a modest salary, but he did not want to work for his father. He told his parents his decision, and they were furious: They had built up a family business and their eldest son refused the gift! Thus my grandfather's Hall Dairy combined with Charlie Brock's Whitneyville Creamery, in September of 1925, to create the Brock-Hall Dairy Company. Cushing Academy hired my father to teach history and coach track, with one or two English courses added—Bette Davis received an A as his student in English—for board, room, and a thousand dollars.

He thrived in the classroom and wanted to teach for the rest of his life, but he wanted even more to marry Lucy. Apparently there were young people in 1926 who permitted themselves lovemaking without marriage—but not Lucy and Don. At the end of a year, fierce with desire and inhibition, they married secretly in Boston, a civil ceremony; Caroline stood up for her sister. The next school year, they sneaked off for weekends, but weekends were insufficient. After two years of teaching—an island paradise that he cherished in memory—my father gave up, quit Cushing, and went to work for his father. He made enough money to support my mother; they could openly marry and set up housekeeping. The ceremony took place in the living room of the farm—and my father suffered the family business until he died.

One year of prep school, after high school, had accomplished the good in my father's life, and he had long planned that I would do what he had done. But early in 1944 it looked as if I would be drafted when I graduated from Hamden High. My father decided that I should go to prep school now, halfway through high school, and not wait until I graduated. He wanted me to go somewhere considered better than Cushing, and he had heard of "Exeter and Andover" as the best schools for boys. (We knew no one acquainted with St. Paul's, St. Mark's, Groton, Milton, or Middlesex.) Because Exeter came first in the phrase "Exeter and Andover," he wrote to Exeter; he never got around to writing Andover. (Exeter mostly led to Harvard, Andover to Yale, but we did not know.) I needed to take exams to be admitted, and was tutored by New Haven high school teachers in mathematics, a subject in which I was always stupid, and in Latin. Hamden High was at that time a dreadful school. I had all A's, even in algebra. (In our enormous math class a bored and cynical teacher had us correct each other's exams; we all had A's.) In Hamden High's sophomore English, I was required to submit one paragraph of writing during the whole year. In Latin, forty-five pupils chanted "*amo, amas, amat*" in unison. At the end of two years at Hamden, Latin students translated twelve lines of Caesar a night. At Exeter, as I discovered the next year, *first*-year Latin students ended by doing *eighty* lines of Caesar a night. When I took the Latin exam for entrance to Exeter, I was asked to translate a passage of Caesar that I had just worked over with my tutor—in my life, one of a thousand crucial pieces of good luck.

Exeter was luck because it made Harvard easy. It was the dysphoric hell that provided access to heaven. Just before my sixteenth birthday, my parents used their saved-up gasoline coupons to drive me to Exeter, in southern New Hampshire not far from the ocean. That year, the academy had taken more students than it had rooms for, so I started as resident of the infirmary annex, a low building of small hospital rooms where students would be housed if the school came down with the flu. There were only six of us, who would be placed in regular dorms when space was available—when somebody flunked out or got sick or was expelled. It was an unfortunate start, to be so separated when I felt lonely and homesick already, but maybe it would have been worse to start in a dorm where everybody knew each other—including boys who had attended Manhattan day schools together and who sailed summers in the Hamptons. Exeter was not only such privileged boys; when I graduated I found that some friends had attended on full scholarships; the families of others drove to graduation in Packards as long as football fields. Exeter was not uppity, but it was a society of cliques, like all boarding schools. I felt alienated from The Boys, as they were called, who looked alike, acted alike, and appeared to think alike. Either they came from similar backgrounds or they faked it.

At the beginning, Exeter was stony loneliness. Walking alone from the infirmary annex to eat dinner, I did not know where I was. I saw a lean boy, who looked as hapless as I felt, and asked him if this building was the dining hall. He wasn't sure. He looked pleased to be spoken to—by someone who felt as estranged as he did. Thus began, out of mutual hopelessness, a great and redeeming friendship. He was Ted Lewis from Washington, son of an AP bureau head who would shortly become a columnist for the *New York Daily News.* Later I would visit him and his family in Alexandria and fall in love for a year with a girl I met there. Later we would hang out together at Harvard, he would be best man when I first married, we would visit with our young families, and he would drop dead when he was fifty-two. In the autumn of 1944 we took walks together, talked about becoming writers, and cherished our separation from the society in which we found ourselves. Before Christmas I moved to a single room (single rooms were rare) in Hoyt Hall. Ted visited and we talked long—when I wasn't in a panic over flunking out.

At chapel—eight every morning, after breakfast—the whole school gathered in a frigid assembly hall, saving on fuel in wartime, to sing hymns, to listen to prayers, and to hear faculty speeches. Every morning I sat shivering, bored, and apprehensive of classes that would follow: "Hall, you seem remarkably unacquainted with the subjunctive." "Hall, go bang your head." My stupid mathematics occasioned a light moment in my first Exeter year. The teacher for our geometry class was Bill Clark, who was football coach, an old Dartmouth halfback known by the affectionate nickname of "Bull." He was red-faced, short-haired, and taught math as if he were charging a matador or a line-backer—but he was also a friendly man who liked to laugh. Because geometry terrified me, I made constant mistakes: I neglected to bring my book; I brought my book but forgot my homework. Bull Clark imposed a standard punishment on students who goofed: He required them to write a poem and bring it next day to class. Again and again for chastisement he made me write a poem—often a sonnet—and again and again I provided him with something rhymed and in lines, which he read aloud at the start of class, beaming broadly and laughing. It was, of course, Bull Clark's notion that writing a poem, for an adolescent boy, was pure torment. Then the *PEA Review*, the school's literary magazine, appeared with a cluster of my poems—none commissioned for class; these were my *poems*—and Bull found it blusteringly funny that he had punished me by requiring me to do what I did anyway. He took such pleasure in telling this story that it may account for my passing his course with a D minus.

At least once a week in chapel we sang the hymn "*Gaudeamus igitur / Iuvenes dum sumus* . . ." I knew just enough Latin to enjoy the irony: "Let us rejoice therefore / While we are young . . ." Let us rejoice to inhabit a province of clones in a country of sarcasm. Of course there were human oases, even besides Ted Lewis, students one at a time who were intelligent and inward and self-sufficient. Harvey Lyon and I remain close. Harvey is a Jew, which made him at Exeter as much an outsider as a socialist poet was. Anti-Semitism was the norm, usually mild in its expression, not always: Another old schoolmate sent me a friendly message through his daughter: "Tell him the Jewboy says hello." In my last year at Exeter there was one Negro student, three years behind me, whom I did not know. One morning he woke up to find pairs of shoes lined up outside his door. Now, when I visit the school called by the same name, I see black faces everywhere, Asian faces, and the faces of females. To a visitor from the planet of antiquity, the Exeter of our moment does not resemble its ancestor.

But I was not satisfied to keep to Ted and Harvey, and a few others, or to become wholly a recluse. Unable simply to ignore The Boys, to live in a separate society of one, I defined myself as their opposite—and thus I was as controlled by them as if I had tried to mimic them. I had publicly to be a poet, and publicly proclaimed myself socialist or maybe communist in this archaic-Republican tidal river. When Roosevelt died that first spring, Exeter students snake-danced until someone near the head of the line cried out, "Oh, my God. Truman!" Meantime I subscribed to the weekly edition of *The Worker*, which I read not in the privacy of my room but in the dormitory's butt room—people smoked in those years—with the tabloid spread open so that its title was impossible to misread.

Shortly after I arrived at Exeter, my mother telephoned. A long envelope had arrived for me addressed in my own handwriting, what we called a "rejection." I had authorized her to open such envelopes. This time, I had a poem accepted for publication—

"Scythe Mowing"—in a magazine called *Trails* that devoted itself to the natural world. My triumph was as intense as any in my adult life, and surely it was the same for my mother. (I found copies of *Trails* when I unpacked her boxes.) At sixteen I was publishing not only in school magazines but in the adult literary world. *Trails* took more poems, and I placed one poem with a magazine called *Matrix* out of Pittsburgh and another with *Experiment* from St. Louis. It took me some time to understand that the magazines were as inferior as my poems. In the *Experiment* poem I wrote, "the night peeled back like a dried scab." How *modern*. The poems I published in the *PEA Review*, always reviewed savagely by the *Exonian*—the student paper, good training—were relentlessly *modern*, and *modern* did not fare well in Exeter's climate.

To fare ill, in Exeter's climate, may have provided ultimate advantage. One famous writer, asked in a *Paris Review* interview to name the grand source of his work, replied, "Revenge!" At Hamden High School, and afterward at Exeter, I suffered the usual taunts—"Go write a poem about it!"—but jeers from fellow adolescents provide insufficient engines for revenge; there must be some grander affront. (Robert Frost said that a poet needs a snout for punishment.) One event of my first year at Exeter was devastating and useful. It was humiliating, and I spoke of it to no one at the time—contrary to my usual habit of telling everything to everybody. I did not tell Leonard Stevens, the rare English teacher who knew and loved modern poetry; I did not tell my parents or Ted Lewis. I was ridiculed in front of peers, about what was most important to me, at a vulnerable moment, by a figure of authority and power. The teacher who administered my shame did it for my own good. Every enormity is performed for the good of its victim.

My classes had been astonishingly difficult. In the first marking period, I had E's—the failing grade—in Latin, geometry, and history. In Latin and mathematics I had been ill prepared. But in *history?* Apparently, I didn't know how to study—whatever that means. As a new student, I had been placed in a slow English class taught by a soccer coach who hung on his wall a holograph poem by Thomas Hardy. (His advocacy delayed my discovery of Hardy's poetry by fifteen years.) I did well enough, and was moved to a more demanding class. I published poems in the school magazine. My only other small Exeter success was marginal participation on the track team, running the 600 in the winter and becoming third man of three in the 440 come spring. At the end of the first semester, I had pulled myself up to a B in English, and my E's in other subjects had elevated themselves to D minuses; therefore I was allowed to return for the winter term. At the same time I learned that there was an elite English class for the brightest third-year students, taught by a man named Chilson Hathaway Leonard, who had a Ph.D. from Yale. He was an imposing figure on campus, above middle height, ample but not fat, with an impassive mien. He was an apostle of wholesomeness. In the afternoons, when most teachers coached something athletic—even the most unlikely faculty lingered limply beside a basketball court—Chilson Hathaway Leonard coached the sport of woodchopping. Much of the faculty—I learned later—found him comic in his celebration of rustic manly virtue, but he was not dumb; his knowledge of literature was considerable. Like

most of his Exeter colleagues, he loathed all contemporary poets except for Robert Frost and Frost's perceived heir Stephen
Vincent Benét. In the thirties and forties, it was not permitted to
admire Eliot and Frost together.

Because of my zeal for eminence, and despite the teacher's
taste in poetry, I applied to be admitted to English 3 Special. My
most recent English teacher recommended me, and C.H.L. read
two or three of my themes. In an interview he allowed that I was
proficient enough for his class; but, he told me, he detested the
poetry I published in the school magazine. It was modern rub-
bish, E. E. Cummings and the rest of them. He paused, looking
stern. "If you want to take my class anyway, you can." Of course I
wanted to, all the more because I was challenged.

It is students, not teachers, who make any class memorable,
and in this special English class the students were smart, united
not by love of literature but by force of intelligence. (Doubtless
many took an elite, Special course—math, Latin—in a subject
that I was flunking.) We read Wordsworth, Thoreau, *Othello*. We
wrote papers. We took tests. I wrote a theme about the Waverly
Inn, reporting the behavior of drunks. The theme came back with
a derisory grade: This subject was nothing for a young American
to write about. When I wrote another paper, about a day spent
chasing wild heifers with my grandfather, I received an A. Toward the middle of the winter term, we were given a free theme:
We could write and submit anything we wished. I knew he meant
prose, but after class I asked him if I might give him poems instead. He looked at me out of his impassive face. "I told you what
I thought of your poetry?" I nodded. "All right," he said, turning
away, "if that's what you want."

When we received the winter's midterm grades, I discovered that my schoolwork had resumed its failure. My Latin dropped back to an E, together with geometry, and this time French rather than history. Again I appeared to be flunking out; I was put on academic probation, which meant that I sat in a study hall every evening. Worse, my grades expelled me from the track team. Just as I learned about my failures, my probation, and my dismissal from track, our English class met for the first time since we had submitted our free themes. Beginning the hour, Chilson Hathaway Leonard told the best students at Exeter that Hall was flunking three courses. (We did not know one another's grades.) He said that Hall was flunking because he wasted his time writing this drivel. He read my poems aloud to the class, and when he had completed each poem he ridiculed it. I remember only one of his remarks, innocuous enough. Concluding a poem, I wrote that no bells rang. The teacher looked up, surveyed the class, and addressed me: "You don't ring the bell?" He read another poem and ridiculed it; he read another. Gathered around the oblong table, the other students laughed. Bright as they were, they were adolescent males; at first they enjoyed the spectacle of my shame. As the hour continued, they quieted. Again and again, they learned that Hall was failing in his studies because he devoted his hours to ludicrous endeavors—like this garbage; like this; like this . . . C.H.L. would not relent, and his performance filled the entire class period. My classmates looked at the floor. I don't know what I looked at, but I remember my rage, and the determination that anger should not show in tears. When the next assignment was given and the class finished, the students filed out. No one spoke. Two or three of my classmates, to my astonishment, patted me on the arm or the shoulder. When I returned to my room my anger flew out in tears. I determined that I would work on my poems until the blood boiled in my veins. I added to love of poetry the power of outrage and the motive of revenge.

In time, I managed to raise my grades, was graduated and admitted to Harvard. Eight years after Mr. Leonard's class I published my first book. Exeter asked me back to read my poems, an evening performance in the chapel. By this time, I was old enough to know that publishing a book, or being praised, does not mean that you are good. Nonetheless, it was satisfying to return in triumph to a scene of defeat. Maybe the prodigal's return would sponsor chagrin in my old teacher? I drove into town and onto the campus with foreboding, simply because Exeter remained associated with anxiety and distress. I checked in with the chairman of the English department and learned that I would be introduced that night by Chilson Hathaway Leonard. I was dumbstruck, and asked why. The chairman told me that when I had been his student, C.H.L. had grumbled to other teachers about me and my poems. When I won Oxford's Newdigate Prize, when my things appeared in *The New Yorker*, when my book received awards, his colleagues teased him. They did not know what he had done in his classroom a decade earlier, and it amused them to invite him to introduce the student he had complained of. For a moment I thought of getting back at him, on the platform, by telling the story of that class. But public retaliation is always repellent. When we met that night, Chilson Hathaway Leonard was genial and offered congratulations; we did not speak of what we both remembered. He introduced me, I read, I departed.

A decade later, I took a revenge that was acceptable because

I didn't intend it. In the *New York Times Book Review* I wrote a short essay on Wordsworth's poem about daffodils, suggesting an unintentional underside to the poem. At the end I asserted that if a reader felt that my reading damaged the poem, then the reader had never cared for the poem anyway, but for some post-card—daffodils blooming in the Lake Country—that an English teacher passed around in class. I remembered nothing of an English teacher and a postcard; I thought I was making up an ex-ample of pedagogic or sentimental literalness. A week later I re-ceived the postcard, a black-and-white photograph of daffodils blooming in the Lake Country, with a note from Chilson Hatha-way Leonard: "I suppose your fingerprints are still on it."

❖

In my concentration on work, I became more content to live apart from the mass of students. There were joys to being an outsider; writing poetry was better than playing hearts in the butt room. Summers on the New Hampshire farm, solitude with the old people was preferable to the regimentation of summer camp. When The Boys came back from holiday in New York and bragged about feeling up girlfriends on holiday from Dana Hall and getting drunk at La Rue's—it sounded like a nightclub that specialized in serving adolescents—I envied their sophistication but I did not try to resemble them. I walked alone out of town on the Swazey Parkway. When the whole school watched a film in the gymnasium on Saturday night, I stayed in my single room, in love with silence and solitude, in love with writing poems. I wrote or tried to write almost every day. At first they were mod-ernist poems, showing that I read Eliot and Stevens, even Cummings for a while. I remember Auden taking me over, how I read everything I could find, and memorized "As I Walked Out One Evening." Reading about Hart Crane in an Untermeyer anthology, I was moved by his suicide and then by the dazzlement of his language. I wrote free verse exclusively, then began to discover the joys of writing in meter. (Maybe I was more affected by Exeter's literary conservatism than I let myself realize.) Those Saturday nights of writing were the happiest time of the week, separate from any group, alone with language and ambition. At this time in my life, when my social experience was limited to Spring Glen, Hamden High, and Exeter, I had no inkling that any society might be pleasurable. In a vulgar wedding of Latin and Greek, I made up a name for my condition. I was "solophiliac."

Complaining about Exeter, I have barely mentioned a huge redemptive good fortune. There was one English teacher—is there always one teacher?—named Leonard Stevens, who with his wife Mary provided me respite from the bleakness. Leonard Stevens loved modern poetry, which isolated him from his colleagues. He was thrilled to find a student with whom he could talk about Yeats, about Hopkins and "The Windhover," about Wallace Stevens. Leonard Stevens had actually met T. S. Eliot. He had played tennis in Rapallo with Ezra Pound (who confided in him that Wall Street spies were watching the game through binoculars). I never took a class with him. He was a master in my dormitory, and when he was checking us in at night I would delay him by talking about what I had been reading. Years later I dedicated a book of poems to Leonard and Mary, and we remained friends until they died. While Leonard and I talked about poetry, Mary and I talked about life; I believe that "life" consisted mostly of girls, love, and sex.

The good thing about Exeter was its academic difficulty. When I survived the first year, I discovered a benignity within Exeter's rigors. At the end of the year I had a C in Latin, which I had raised not from a mere E but from something like a three out of a hundred. At Prize Day that year, I shared a cash prize, for "Improvement in Latin," with a student who had climbed from a C to an A. My $12.50 was hard earned.

During that first year, there was another teacher who mattered to me, a quiet bachelor named Hyde Cox, who hung an Andrew Wyeth painting in his dormitory living room. He was a temporary hire, filling in until regular instructors returned from the war; he left Exeter the next year. Hyde Cox loved poetry, especially Robert Frost, whom he knew, but he was not limited to Frost. He loaned me his copy of William Carlos Williams's *The Wedge*, my first Williams. He told me about Bread Loaf, the two-week summer writers' conference (first of thousands) in which Frost took desultory part each August. When he told me about it, Bread Loaf became a hill to climb. I persuaded my parents to send me there, at the age of sixteen—if Bread Loaf would accept my application. One could go as an Auditor, listening to lectures, readings, workshops—and keeping one's mouth shut. If one attended as a Contributor, a professional writer would examine one's work in private conference, and one would expose one's work to the publicity of a workshop. Although Contributors were generally in their thirties or forties, I applied as a Contributor. I had a quick note from the assistant director, offering me unpaid employment as a waiter, with the freedom to attend public literary events. Waiters were college students, older than me, and I should have been flattered, but I answered, with sixteen-year-old hauteur, that I would attend as a Contributor or not at all. I was accepted as a Contributor—Hyde Cox must have been responsible—and arrived in August of 1945, after the bombs had been dropped, bringing with me part of a novel, several short stories, and many poems.

My first night, I *saw* Robert Frost, the flesh of a poet. Theodore Morrison was director, later my teacher at Harvard, who was husband to Katherine, who was Frost's secretary and mistress. A novelist and a magazine writer each did prose workshops, and Louis Untermeyer—anthologist of H.D.—workshopped poetry. When my poems were made public, the workshoppers were gentle. Robert Frost, who was not always gentle, did not attend the workshop that day. I spoke with him several times, never about my own work. I sat with him for an hour on the porch of the Bread Loaf Inn with a mother—author of *Pat the Bunny*—and her daughter, who was about to enter Bryn Mawr. Frost was lively, funny, clearly pleased to show off for a beautiful eighteen-year-old. He spoke of his ambivalence about colleges; he couldn't do with them and he couldn't do without them—"sort of like Louis, with women." (Untermeyer had married several times.)

Other writers visited Bread Loaf briefly; I remember talking at length with Richard Wright. I met a student from Colombia who recited Lorca in Spanish and improvised translations. Besides faculty at Bread Loaf there were fellows, brought to the conference on scholarship, writers of one book perhaps, or of a book accepted but not yet published. A. B. Guthrie was a fellow, author of *The Big Sky*, which had not yet appeared. A woman from New York, a novelist and member of the Communist Party, gave me political instruction. A fellow invited me, one evening after

a reading, to visit the cottage of the fellows' privilege. Some id-
iot offered me a drink. When I accepted, I was handed a glass of
straight bourbon. Not to be condescended to, I drank it straight
down, after which a number of fellows walked me up and down,
up and down, hoping I might be persuaded out of a coma. A day or
so later I went back to the fellows' cottage in the evening without
being asked. The faculty, I found out years later, had a meeting at
which they discussed expelling me. They didn't, thank goodness.
My chief bad behavior was chasing. I propositioned woman after
woman, and women were omnipresent; young men remained in
the Pacific or Europe. I was anomalous at Bread Loaf because of
gender as well as age.

On V-J Day, the management decreed that we would spend that
evening in a memorial service of thanksgiving. When we heard
the announcement, I was talking to an attractive blond woman,
twenty-four years old, whose husband was an officer in Germany. She and I were too sophisticated for memorial services,
so we slipped away to a cabin beyond the tennis courts. Surely,
I had sex in mind; maybe she did too. I lamented my virginity
and claimed that I would employ the services of a prostitute. She
objected; I should find a *nice* girl instead. I said that nice girls
didn't do it. She said she had done it, before she was married.
After hours of necking, she became the nice girl she recommended, and V-J Day at Bread Loaf has been framed like a
painting, in the fleshy museum of memory, for sixty years.

A month after Bread Loaf I returned to Exeter—tense with
misgiving, stomach clenched—for my second and senior year.
I would enter Latin 4, I would continue French. Desperate to
avoid chemistry or biology or physics, I opted for a classical di-

ploma, which meant that I could avoid science entirely by taking five years of Latin and Greek in combination. Thus I added to my vestigial Latin a year of beginning Greek. My grades improved, largely to C's. Exeter teachers made a fetish of grade deflation. A C at Exeter was at least a B at Harvard; a B was certainly an A. My English teacher this year was a grave, theatrical, learned man. At the start I did well, with some A's on exams and papers. He asked me to stay after class. "Hall, I have taught here eighteen years. In that time I have given three A's. On several occasions I have taken a lad aside and told him that, if he worked with especial diligence, he might receive an A. I am doing that with you, Hall." My final grade was a B, but Mr. Finch's suggestion was a flattering academic tribute.

Although work was no longer desperate, I still found Exeter cold and depressing. I closed the door of my room and wrote poems. I read books. To go with "solophiliac" I added "bibliomaniac." When I found a new poet—I remember Kenneth Fearing—I would borrow all his books from the school library, and more from the town library, and read him straight through. Except for H.D., a poet was a *him*. The true Emily Dickinson had not appeared; I found Marianne Moore a year later, and Elizabeth Bishop awaited down the road. In fiction I read Henry James and the Russians. I read ten books at a time, piled in stacks by my bed, twenty pages of one, then twenty pages of another. Earlier, I had prided myself on reading with increasing rapidity, counting the pages I ran through in an hour. Now I learned to read more slowly, adjusting to the difficulty or excellence of the language. If you read Henry James as fast as you read James T. Farrell, you do not read Henry James. I read the Great Writers with a capitalized, acquisitive joy, adding to my life list. I would know *all* of Tolstoy. I assumed that reading trash was lighthearted amusement, a vacation from literature and high art. At the end of the term, I would relax on the train ride home by reading Damon Runyon. By the time the train had reached Providence, I was bored by Damon Runyon, and I realized, with a sense of loss: Reading literature had destroyed my enjoyment of junk. John Marcher expelled Hercule Poirot.

Before Christmas I clerked for a week at Judd's, which was New Haven's genteel old bookstore. Miss Judd had inherited the store from her father and ran it in his spirit, recommending new books to a clientele of New Haven gentry. She was a bulwark of a woman in her fifties, formidable and kind and formal, in favor of good literature and propriety. I had patronized her store, along with Yale bookstores not far away, from an early age. My salary during Christmas rush translated itself into books, for Judd's shelves contained marvels. Did Judd's ever return a book to a publisher? Its bookshelves were deep, and a row of old books hid behind each row of current books. I found a 1938 *New Directions* annual, $1.75, and first editions of the ill-selling William Faulkner. Working beside Miss Judd was a small man her age, the bachelor Mr. Kronish, who had read everything and loved to talk about books. He had worked for Miss Judd for twenty years and they addressed each other as "Miss Judd" and "Mr. Kronish."

Late on an afternoon just before Christmas—December 22, 1945—my mother telephoned me at the bookstore: My father had hemorrhaged a third of his blood and was in New Haven Hospital. I hurried there. He was dead white, my mother by his side. He had been having stomach pains in November and a doctor had X-rayed him, looking for a cause, but the picture had not revealed his duodenal ulcer. For a while he was in danger; he recovered and my mother brought him home. When I returned to Exeter, the dairy gave him sick leave and sent my parents to Florida for two weeks. Soon my father felt better than he had before the hemorrhage. For years he had waked every night with a cough, unable to lie down without furies of deep coughing. My mother sat with him and rubbed his head for an hour before the cough subsided and they would go back to sleep. Now with the bleeding ulcer he stopped smoking and the cough went away. The message was clear. But in 1946 the back pages of magazines still photographed male models in doctor costumes who recommended that you smoke Old Golds for your health. After they returned from Florida and my father went back to his desk at Brock-Hall, he took up his Chesterfields again, four packs a day, and the cough came back.

That autumn of 1945, before my father's hemorrhage, I had begun to endure migraine headaches, each of which lasted a few days. Pain started in the left side of the back of my head, sometimes shooting over the scalp into my left eyeball. These episodes were debilitating; I could not read or study. When the pain was at its worst I vomited, and in winter term the headaches became more frequent. Regularly I checked myself into the infirmary. My French teacher, noting the periodicity of my absences, spoke to the class of "Hall's monthlies." Nurses noted that I also ran a low-grade fever. I stayed in an Exeter infirmary bed for two weeks in February, headaches every day, until, on the advice of the school doctor, my parents drove up from Connecticut and took me home. I was seventeen, and my senior year aborted.

Ardmore Street was paradisal: My mother made me milk-shakes, and I lay in bed all day reading and writing. Besides the poems, I took the time to write a novel, *The Loves of Hilary Smart*, which has never suffered the indignity of print. (I found it in the boxes.) When I ran out of books to read, my mother took a bus to the Yale Co-op in New Haven and bought me more. As my symptoms continued, I was admitted to Saint Raphael's Hospital for observation. Doctors suspected mononucleosis, but nothing showed in my blood; they worried about a brain tumor, and did a spinal tap. In the hospital, the student nurses paid me gratify-ing attention. On the floor, I was the only male under sixty. One tall girl was soulful and I pined for her; she became pregnant and left nursing school. Another dark-haired beauty organized a pizza party shortly before I left, climbing up the fire escape and through the window with a large ah-*beats* for the other girls and me. Chatting with me in my room, she told me how she made it a practice to keep three boyfriends going at once. There was a current number one, bracketed by a former front-runner whom she was easing out and a third who would replace the moment's favorite. Even more appealing than the nurses, and more think-able, was a sixteen-year-old candy striper who pushed a broom after high school, a slight, pretty girl named Marie who lingered cleaning my room to talk and josh. When I left the hospital I had her telephone number.

No one ever diagnosed or defined my illness. Shortly before my departure from Saint Raphael's I was visited by a famous doc-tor who specialized in glandular disorders. "Mr. Hall, you remain a mystery." I returned home to bed, to reading, to writing poems and my novel, to my mother's attention—to the daily headache, and to a daily temperature that rarely reached a hundred. Was I a mystery? None of the doctors I saw was a psychiatrist. At Exeter I had been miserable, a condition sometimes called depression. My bodily symptoms were painful, but doctors found nothing wrong with my body. My reward for becoming ill was to leave lonely Exeter and return to my attentive mother, who kept me in books and blank paper—the same mother I had lost to her sickness when I was small. I was restored to childhood, subject to her entire devotion and care. Doubtless such retrogressions are common enough. I know of two other men who lost a high school year to sickness, returned to their mothers—and later got on with their lives. Both were writers, John Fowles and James Wright. At some point in June, although my headaches and fevers persisted, a general practitioner suggested that I get out of bed, throw away the thermometer, and forget that I was sick. So "I decided to live." The headaches diminished. When I took my temperature again, months later, it was normal.

That summer I spent fewer weeks in New Hampshire. I took a job at the Yale Library, for sixty cents an hour, cataloguing uncatalogued periodicals, to fill in for the regular cataloguer during his summer vacation. I stayed in Connecticut not to make sixty cents an hour but to date Marie, as I began my first long romance at seventeen. We dated for three years, until my sophomore year at college. We spoke dreamily of marriage and named our children. She was bright and affectionate and Catholic, from a section of New Haven where her working-class family lived in a triple-decker. Borrowing my parents' car, I drove us to the shore on weekends, occasionally to roadhouses or dances on Saturday nights. We necked endlessly, and never went all the way. This ro-

mance was central to my growing up, because it allowed me un-
alienated entrance into the era's American adolescence—kissing, parking among other cars full of couples kissing, going to
dances at pavilions with big bands, enduring painful hours of
lover's nuts.

My third year at Exeter, my second senior year, was less difficult than the first two. I was a year older and no longer afraid
of flunking out. Marie took the train to big Exeter dances once
a term. Some of my tormentors had graduated, and now at Exeter there were eight veterans of World War II who became my
friends—twenty-one- and twenty-two-year-olds, back from the
Marines or the Army. Because they had been to war they were
older than their ages, and as grown-ups they had no use for the
adolescent polloi. One former Marine from California—who
used "like" as an expletive in 1946—became a roommate at Harvard. Another veteran, known as the only married student at Exeter, took every weekend away, a privilege rarely granted. Later
I discovered that he had not been married at all. He had a girlfriend and lied persuasively to Dean Kerr; or maybe Dean Kerr
was not so naïve as I imagined. I was disgruntled to put off college for another year, but the delay turned out to be fortunate.
When I got to college, my classes were lively with veterans, and
I studied biology or metaphysical poetry sitting next to twenty-
five-year-olds who had been captains of infantry in Italy. It was
good to be a year older.

Soon after I returned to Exeter I made a disagreeable discovery. I had belonged to Exeter's literary club, the Lantern Society,
which occasionally brought in a visiting writer. I remember David McCord, John O'Hara. I belonged because, if you published

enough in the *PEA Review,* membership was automatic. When I returned the rules had changed. Membership was no longer automatic for *Review* writers, the change was retroactive, and I was no longer a member of the Lantern Club. A board of students elected members now, and they had not elected me. I was outraged; no other Exeter student was quite so literary—but the club had become more social than literary. I called on the new president, who reeked of privilege. When I protested, he allowed that the board would consider my application at its next meeting. As I turned in fury to leave, I heard myself snarl—astonished at my rage of *ressentiment*—"Rich boy!"

Admitted to Harvard for the next year, I was graduated from Exeter in the spring of 1947. To my surprise, I was elected class poet. I delivered graduation verses written in the simplest language I could manage—not *modern*—because my verse had a burden: "Let's never forget how miserable we were in this place!" I knew that I spoke for myself, and not for everyone. Still, at my fiftieth reunion I was asked to talk to the portion of my class who were still alive and who chose to return. I began by saying that I had loathed Exeter. "How many of you also hated it?" Despite the distortions of the years, and the self-selection of reunioners, a remarkable number of hands lifted in the stale air of an old dining room. *Gaudeamus igitur / Senectutes dum sumus.*

Homecoming

IN SEPTEMBER OF 1947 I carried suitcases into a suite in Matthews Hall, in the Harvard Yard where freshmen live. My parents had driven me up from Connecticut, the first day I could move in, and we unpacked books, clothes, and a record player. My father stopped over to the Harvard Coop and bought a beer mug with an H on it, and a crimson banner embroidered HARVARD. I thanked him grimly; I knew these objects gave off the wrong tone. When my parents left, I was independent as I had never been before. Such liberty was thrilling. I investigated my rooms, constructed in the nineteenth century for a pair of Brahmins—two bedrooms and a living room. Three of us would live here in 1947, and because I arrived early I secured the smaller, single bedroom. When my roommates arrived, we were shy with each other. One was from Andover, and the other had graduated from high school in Muskegon, Michigan. I was eighteen, almost nineteen, and a representative easterner in my stereotypical geographic snobbery: If you come from the South you are dumb; if you come from California you are a kook; if you come from the Midwest you are boring, naïve, and Republican. Because I was a liberal, I took pains to be helpful to my Muskegon roommate. I did everything but show him which fork to use. For my pains, I would live as an adult for seventeen years in Michigan.

The dorm filled up. Other rooms on our entry held high

schoolers from Tennessee, preppies from Taft and Governor Dummer, and two African Americans. Wherever we came from, we had much in common. I had found my own generation at last. In my first weeks, even the most ordinary event was extraordinary. I remember an epiphanic gathering in our living room, in the first week of freshman year. Ten or twelve strangers, eighteen years old, sat together and began tentative acquaintance. There was a boy from a high school in Kansas, another from St. Paul's. As we chatted, someone mentioned poetry; doubtless it was me. No one spoke with scorn, no one made a gagging sound, no one mimed effeminacy. One by one, each of us mentioned a favorite poem. Someone recited Kipling's "If." I have no idea whom I spoke of—maybe Yeats by that time.

Because I was excused by examination from taking freshman composition, I could enroll in an elementary creative writing class. Creative writing had little presence in colleges then. (At Iowa, there was something called a Writers' Workshop.) Harvard offered three courses in writing, each practicing all genres. I took the beginning English C, and my teacher was John Ciardi, one of the bright young poets in a school of wit led by Karl Shapiro, who had won a Pulitzer Prize for *V-Letter and Other Poems* (1944). These poets wrote ingenious stanzas about common objects: Shapiro wrote "Buick"; John Frederick Nims made a poem meticulously describing a dollar bill. John Ciardi's *Other Skies* had recently appeared to critical praise, a collection mostly out of his Air Force years in the Pacific. We admired "Elegy Just in Case": "Here lie Ciardi's pearly bones, / In their ripe organic mess. / Jungle blown, his chromosomes / Breed to a new address." Ciardi's poems regularly appeared in *The New Yorker*.

He was handsome, powerful, with a black mustache and straight bright black hair, of which a great swatch regularly fell across his forehead—"insured for ten thousand bucks"—and two afternoons a week he plunged like a fullback into the classroom, his Harvard green book bag slung over his shoulder. He was shrewd and sharp, demanding enough, and praised with a generous authority. In politics, he was famously liberal or even radical, and in class we heard political bulletins. At the Progressive Party's convention in Shibe Park, in 1948, he would give the fundraising address. Henry Wallace was nominated for president with a policy that advocated closer relations with the Soviet Union—an alternative to Dewey the Republican and Truman the Democrat. Ciardi's voice was dark, low, and resonant, and he knew well how to play upon it, which was perhaps why he was chosen to speak at the convention. He used The Voice reading our poems aloud, and when taking attendance.

Later he used it lecturing from coast to coast, and the young poet turned into a public face of poetry. He earned good money addressing conventions of teachers or anybody else—charming, charismatic, and increasingly rich. He wrote a popular textbook, *How Does a Poem Mean?*, and became poetry editor of the *Saturday Review of Literature*. There, he denounced Anne Morrow Lindbergh's poetry, and was berated by middlebrows. His timid *Saturday Review* editor wrote an editorial that apologized for John's opinions, John noisily resigned, the editor capitulated, and Ciardi signed on to do more lectures. After Theodore Morrison, Ciardi directed Bread Loaf, a position that would become a castle of influence; whoever has preference to bestow receives preference in return. As his wealth increased so did his girth, while his poetry and his literary reputation lapsed downward. He had grown up poor, working nights in North Station while he was in high school, and he remained astonished by his own wealth. He became his money's victim. John, who had been kind and intelligent and left wing, became a landlord and a braggart about money, a caricature of greed. I remember how, one day in 1947, he strode into class and said in The Voice: "I just sold eight poems to *The New Yorker* and bought my first new car. Next time I'll vote Republican." Beware the jokes you make when you are young.

For me that fall, Ciardi's English C was thrilling—a huddle of young men who would be writers. I wrote nothing then that I would want to keep, but I worked hard and joined in the enthusiasm and energy of people my own age who were ambitious like me. The class was especially lively at the front of the room, left-hand side, where two students sat together. One was tall, lank, chinless, who seemed to have been assembled without bones, called Ted Gorey, who became Edward St. John Gorey, the artist, set designer, and writer of limericks, possessed of a morbid, funny, camp manner, whose admirers included Edmund Wilson. Beside him sat his roommate, Frank O'Hara, who was short, compact, a Navy veteran, effeminate, and gifted with acerb wit. He wrote short stories in the manner of Ronald Firbank, and stood out in class for a quickness and sophistication that left me admiring and terrified. In the first week of my first term, this small prodigious man was literary Harvard. Later, I lived in Eliot House where Frank and Ted had their rooms; they gave the best parties: talk, talk, talk. With other poets and actors we drank beer together at Cronin's and hung out at the Mandrake Book Store, which provided free coffee and plentiful gossip.

When you call someone witty, it is hard to come up with an example that proves the point. Once I made some teasing comparison of Frank with Oscar Wilde, and Frank turned on me. *"You're the type that would sue!"* After Frank's early death, Ted Berrigan and I were talking about him, and I complained that I could never think of an adequate example of his wit. Ted told me a representative anecdote. When Frank lived in New York—writing poems, working for the Museum of Modern Art, drinking—and attended parties, he suffered from handsome young admirers, straight, who hung around him just out of touching range. Ted remembered a party where everybody talked about movies, and one of Frank's heterosexual acolytes described a film of which he could not remember the title. Whenever conversation paused, the young man returned to the subject, insinuated details of the film, and kept asking, "What is it called? What *is* the title?" Finally Frank answered, with the emphatic delivery that underscored his payoff lines, *"The Bore!"*

Postwar Harvard for two or three years was left wing in politics and open about homosexuality, long before Stonewall. I remember seeing Frank walking outdoors holding hands with a friend. In my flirtation with the left, which had been so useful at Exeter, I joined the John Reed Club, devoted to Marxist discussion and argument. I made a number of communist friends, and was asked to join the party. I went to hootenannies; I was told—a recruitment incentive—that a party member would have greater success with girls than a mere fellow traveler. I remember walking the streets of Cambridge one night, four hours of relentless talk with a communist friend who exhorted me to join his cell. I liked the man and was tempted, but caution or fear (not political intelligence) held me back. Many years later, while the Cold War was thriving, I met the same man when I read poems at his university. I asked him if he remembered that long night's walk and his argument that I join him in the party. He gave me a blank look. There had been no such walk, he told me, and no such conversation; he had never belonged to the party.

In 1947, local cells devised programs to bring waverers into the struggle. I was asked to join a group called Cambridge Citizens in Support of the Strikers at Squires' Meat Packing Plant. Most of us were graduate students or wives of graduate students; I was the token freshman and felt like an ass. One Saturday we made placards indicating our support, and marched carrying our signs to the plant where workers were picketing. We tried to join the line. A union boss restrained us. He told us, warily, that our help was appreciated but not needed. "The boys are a little jumpy today," he said. Communists would do the cause no good.

In the fall of my sophomore year, when Henry Wallace's Progressive Party struggled by petition to put its name on Massachusetts ballots, I knocked on doors in South Boston. The election that November changed my politics, as it did for many others. The favorite was the Republican Thomas E. Dewey, bland governor of New York, who in his campaign continually revealed that "the future lies before us." He ran against Harry Truman, Roosevelt's successor, who had dropped the bombs on Japan and who confronted Soviet expansionism. Everyone knew that Dewey would win; *Life* published his portrait with the caption "The Next President of the United States." One reason for Republican certainty was that the Wallace campaign would take votes away from Truman. Election Day, Harvard's Republican Club rented Memorial

Hall and stocked it with cases of champagne. In an early edition the *Chicago Daily Tribune* published its famous headline—DEWEY DEFEATS TRUMAN—which Truman held up the next day for photographers. Truman's plain roughness, compared to the slick Dewey, touched millions of Americans. At the time, I was taking a lecture course in public opinion, given by a professor who in his Monday lecture explained with scientific precision, using figures from polls, why Dewey was bound to win. The professor's next lecture was a masterpiece of chagrin. Like many people who voted that day—I was not yet twenty-one—I found myself suddenly turned Truman supporter. When his election became clear late in the evening, a crowd of Trumanites gathered in the Yard and marched on the Young Republicans in Memorial Hall—a desolate scene of morose YRs lounging about in formal wear among unopened bottles of champagne. Champagne flowed, not into Republican gullets.

If I could switch so easily from Wallace to Truman, how deep could my socialism go? My politics was a reaction to my Connecticut father and grandfather, who during Roosevelt's presidency spoke of "that man in the White House, who had never met a payroll." After Truman's election, or maybe the Wallace debacle, my leftism faded into rote liberalism. For a while, Brahmins continued to hawk the *Daily Worker* on the street, but later came the House Un-American Activities Committee, the Korean War, and Senator Joseph McCarthy. Before I graduated, the Harvard tone had begun to turn high Episcopal and conservative. In Eliot House, a chapel appeared in the cellar. Communists and homosexuals returned to the closet and the underground.

My Harvard was a paradise of poets and theater. These years

were not the best of my life, heaven knows, but they were the first
years of my best life. Harvard was also frightening—these folks
were smart!—but my fear was more stimulating than debilitating;
it was good to swim with the sharks. When Harvard folk spoke
of an acquaintance, two sentences were permitted for starters:
"He's rather bright" or "He's not very bright." Tormentors from
Exeter disappeared, replaced by intelligentsia from the farms
of Minnesota, the suburbs of Cincinnati, and the Bronx High
School of Science. Many prep school boys vanished into socially
elite clubs like Porcellian and Fly, institutions that were essential
to the Harvard of thirty years before, when there were no houses
like Eliot. Now they had become peripheral; I did not know—my
friends did not know—which buildings housed which clubs.

My club was the *Harvard Advocate*, a literary magazine that appeared six times a year. As soon as I knew of the *Advocate*, I determined to become an editor. The magazine held competitions for
the editorial board once a term. I skipped the competition in the
fall of freshman year in order to concentrate on beginning college. In winter term I enrolled myself as a candidate, seeking admission from editors—all male, as they would be in 1948—who
did not smile, who were older than I was, who were terrifying.
A candidate made public judgments on submitted manuscripts
and was required to do housework. When Robert Lowell tried out
in 1936, he performed janitorial duties, tacking carpets, before
he failed election and transferred to Kenyon College. In 1948 I
painted woodwork; I was incompetent. At gatherings with editors, candidates talked or argued about contemporary literature
and about the manuscripts we had read. On a final night we were
interviewed, and in our absence voted on.

The magazine began in 1866, founded, as its name suggests, in a combative, not a literary, capacity. Among the undergraduates who wrote in its pages were two presidents named Roosevelt. Eventually the magazine became literary, and in 1948 its bound volumes included the juvenilia of E. A. Robinson, T. S. Eliot, E. E. Cummings, Conrad Aiken, and Wallace Stevens. (In my junior year, when I was literary editor, John Ciardi, representing a publisher, asked me to collect an anthology from the magazine, printing early work of the lately eminent. A year later *The Harvard Advocate Anthology* appeared, the first book with my name on its cover.) Voted in, I joined an editorial board that included John Ashbery, Robert Bly, and Kenneth Koch. The novelists Harold Brodkey and Louis Begley were elected later. Members who did not turn out to be writers became editors or journalists—and Daniel Ellsberg decades later photocopied documents belonging to the Rand Corporation. It was Robert Bly I met first, and he has remained my dearest friend, from an evening when we collided and talked about Robert Lowell and Richard Wilbur. He was rather bright, you might say, and otherwise he was a Robert Bly who would be unrecognizable now. A veteran of the Navy (whom I took to be twenty-five; he had just turned twenty-two), he was always serious and spoke barely opening his mouth. He wore a three-piece suit and a narrow striped tie, and advised me to wear more conservative neckwear. At first I knew him as a critic, and his demeanor was critical. Within a year he was Bob Bly the poet. He dropped the Harvard manner and wardrobe, wore checkered shirts, and laughed out loud. He and I spent hundreds of hours together, talking poetry, reading each other's things, tirelessly critical, rewriting each other's work. In those first years we talked constantly of Yeats and quoted him at each other. We wrote poems that suggested an Irish ancestry. We also took lessons from the new young poets, Bly from the pentameters of Robert Lowell in *Lord Weary's Castle,* and I from the elegant stanzas of Richard Wilbur. We saw each other every day. After college we continued to visit each other—in Minnesota, in Michigan, in New York, in New Hampshire, at various poetry occasions—as well as writing each other something like twenty thousand letters. Fifty-odd years later, this friendship endures at the center of our lives. By this time we have shown each other our poems—celebrating and damning, writing lines for each other—from the '40s into the '00s.

Frank O'Hara never joined the *Advocate.* He published there, and knew many editors. Adrienne Rich and I were in the same class, and the *Advocate* had the sense to publish her, but she was female and therefore could not be an editor. I first heard her name through Robert Bly. Radcliffe held a series of dances called jolly-ups where the Harvards and the Radcliffes met one another. Bly returned from a jolly-up telling me that he had found "a girl from Baltimore . . . father's a surgeon . . . knows all about modern po-etry." Later, Adrienne and I double-dated with Robert and one of Adrienne's Radcliffe friends. We drank beer together in Cronin's, and the second date was a disaster. I drank much beer; showing off, I was rude to Bob. When I took Adrienne back to her dormi-tory I attempted to kiss her; she swerved her head so that my lips brushed her cheek. A few years later, Adrienne and I became close friends and lived with our spouses back in Cambridge; we worked together on poems as Robert and I did. Only a decade or two ago, I met Robert's old date, in Boston, now a businesswoman and Democratic fundraiser. When she identified herself I asked her if she remembered what we had talked about, those nights in a booth at Cronin's. "Well," she told me, "you and Robert and Adrienne said your poems . . ." I guess she accepted her role.

Kenneth Koch was a leader on the *Advocate* — outspoken, sophisticated, intelligent, well read, brash, and combative. He had been in the Army, and was as confirmed a poet as anyone. One night after I was elected, the editorial board took a poem of mine for printing, my first in the *Advocate*. Koch was not present, and the next day, when I bumped into him on the street, I told him about my good fortune. He told me that my poem would never have made it had he been at the meeting. Koch's particular admiration on the *Advocate* was John Ashbery, another young man whose life was already poetry. Bly and I wrote vatic, thundering poems, loving Yeats and blarney. Koch and Ashbery (and O'Hara) were devoted to W. H. Auden. Differing tastes agreed on one matter, which was the excellence of John Ashbery, who had published in *Poetry* while he was at Deerfield Academy. He was quiet and reticent then, seldom stating his opinion or even speaking, but we were aware of his cranky intelligence and humor. We published his poems as often as we could. In John's last year, we were pasting together an issue and found ourselves short half a page. I addressed John: "Come on, we haven't printed a poem by you for ages. You know you've got one in your room; go get it for us." John demurred; he had nothing. We teased, he demurred, we teased. Finally he agreed that he *might* have something, and slouched away toward his Dunster House. He returned in fifteen minutes with a brief poem beginning, "Fortunate Alphonse, the shy homosexual . . ." We were enthusiastic and pasted the typescript into the issue. A week later I had a notion: "John," I asked, "did you walk back to Dunster and write that poem?" He admitted it. Forty years later, in the '90s, I saw him in New York and repeated this story, to see if he remembered it as I did. He recited further lines of the poem, never reprinted, and sighed. "Yes. I took longer then."

Although we gave tea parties for visiting poets—our tea was martinis—and although after one editorial meeting we adjourned to the Old Howard, a burlesque house in Scollay Square, we were an ambitious bunch. We argued late into the night about whether a poem was good enough to go into an issue. Was it up to our standards? We never came to blows, but there were hard feelings. As I look back at what we printed in those issues, it's hard to determine what our standards were. Surely we published some terrible poems. To speak of late-night furious arguments over acceptance or rejection is to suggest how self-important we were—and I don't regret it. We took ourselves seriously and we took literature seriously; we learned from our arguments. Our attitude toward print was continuous with attitudes of the old poets. In the twenty-first century—with its proliferation of certified poets grasping M.F.A.s, with the omnipresence of poetry readings and karaoke poets at the open mike, with cheap printing sponsoring a multiplicity of magazines and presses—it is hard to remember how numerically small was the 1950s poetic endeavor, and in contrast how sublime or pretentious was its ambition. We wanted, like Keats, to be among the English poets when we died. The name of poet was glorious for us, as it was for Milton. Shakespeare and Jonson and Dryden wanted to write lines or epics that would live forever. Maybe I should whisper it—it was naïve and perhaps farcical in its self-regard—but so did we.

There was also life outside the *Advocate*. There were even courses in the study of literature. I avoided science, math, economics. I avoided history, which has become a late passion of mine. I avoided music. I avoided the study of art, and only started to look at pictures in my junior year, when an Edvard Munch show arrived at the Fogg Art Museum. Mostly I avoided fiction, in my Honors English major, and took seminars in seventeenth-century poetry, and in the criticism of poetry. As a freshman I had sought and received admission to a class taught by F. O. Matthiessen in which he attended to four poets, beginning with Chaucer and continuing with Pope, Keats, and Yeats. He asked for a show of hands: Who was unfamiliar with Chaucer's language? Three or four of us put our hands up. Well, said Matthiessen, then we don't need to study Chaucer's language.

Matthiessen—socialist, Christian, homosexual—killed himself the following year. Maybe the Cold War killed him. During a lecture one afternoon he was noticeably irritable. Someone coughed, and Matthiessen paused. After a second cough he approached the student with cough drops. "I can't lecture over this noise." When he concluded, he left the room but immediately returned. He apologized for his snappishness and said that we would understand the cause when we learned "of the death by suicide of Jan Masaryk." Matthiessen had just spent a term in Prague and had returned praising the democratic socialism of Czechoslovakia. Foreign Minister Masaryk committed suicide or was murdered by defenestration, and Matty seemed to make reference to Masaryk when he leapt a year later from a high floor of the Hotel Manger, a seedy establishment next to North Station. The day his suicide made newspaper headlines, I heard at lunch a remark that was emblematic of another (legendary and revolting) Harvard. A tutor at Eliot House wagged his eyebrows and asked with distaste, "But *why* did he choose the *Manger?*"

Later I took a full year of Chaucer and discovered the Scots Chaucerians, especially Henryson and Dunbar, whom I continue to read. I took a year's course in "English Theater from Its Ritual Origins to the Closing of the Theaters," from Harry Levin, and also his "Proust, Joyce, and Mann." (In the final exam, the last question had us analyze a passage of Proust's French or of Mann's German or of Joyce's *Wake;* I chose Proust.) To avoid hard science, I took Natural Sciences 5, which was commonly nicknamed "Cocktail Biology." The lecturer set the tone at the beginning of the class by asking, in a lackadaisical manner, "What *is* life, anyway?" We never came up with an answer, but touched on topics within biology: embryology, photosynthesis, evolution . . . In something called a lab, I killed a frog. I earned merely a C in this class, but many poems crawled out of its subject matter.

Tutorial was automatic for people taking honors in English. My sophomore year, Walter Jackson Bate tutored me. He was a good teacher—I took his "Age of Johnson" course, and another in Keats—and next year for tutorial he booted me upstairs to the professor he most admired, who was Harry Levin. My junior and senior years, I spent an hour a week alone with Levin. Admiring and fearing him, I worked hard for tutorial. Levin frightened me partly because of his almost debilitating shyness. When I signed on with him each term, he could not look me in the eye, but stared at the floor and mumbled that it would be an honor . . . for him . . . to have me . . . take tutorial with him . . . for another term. I left his office weak in the knees. Levin's memory allowed him to tutor without preparation. Each week I named an author to work up for the following week. When I chose Tennyson, I read almost all the poems, and a biography, and some criticism, but when Levin asked me what I thought of "Maud," I had not read it. His demeanor froze and he said nothing; I never came to tutorial again without having read my author through. Levin was a professor of comparative literature, and had never done a Ph.D.; instead, he did two three-year terms as a junior fellow in Harvard's Society of Fellows, where young scholars of comparative literature or logic or psychology or physics or musicology or law or biology undergo three years of absolute liberty (no teaching, no course work) to pursue learning and invention. At twenty-six, as a junior fellow, he wrote a brief book about Joyce, which included in fifty pages an introduction and guide to *Ulysses* that remains exemplary. His work was more historical and referential than the prevailing New Criticism; his range was broad, his allusions multiform.

My Chaucer professor was B. J. Whiting—funny, dour, and misogynist—who devoted his attention to the words of Chaucer, not to the ideas that might be derived from them. On the final he included one essay question, for instance about the Great Chain of Being, and devoted the rest of the three hours to spot passages, perhaps a hundred, none so long as a whole line. Some good graduate students had difficulty passing the course—a C was failure—because they read the poetry for ideas and implications, as if *The Canterbury Tales* were a text for study of the late Middle Ages. I read for the words, and did not miss an identification. In more intellectual courses, I struggled. Douglas Bush lectured on Milton and I managed a B.

All medievalists who specialize in Chaucer are funny like

Whiting. When Levin was an undergraduate, Whiting was his tutor, a major conflict of sensibilities. Levin told me a story. One week he chose William Blake to study. He reread Blake, went to the Fogg to look at its collection of Blake graphics, read the critics, reread Blake again. When the tutorial started, Whiting asked Levin what he thought of Blake. In his enthusiasm Levin talked about Blake without pause for twenty minutes while Whiting addressed his pipe. When he ended, Whiting interjected, "All right, but what's wrong with Blake?" Levin said that perhaps, in the later prophetic books, Blake was so private and arcane that the writing was obscure. "Yes," said Whiting, "but what's *wrong* with Blake?" I don't remember what Harry came up with, but he found a second possible debility in the poet. "Yes, but what's *wrong* with Blake?" (All jokes come in three parts.) Levin told Whiting that he gave up, and Whiting answered his own question: "He's bats," he said.

Bullshitting at Cronin's was integral to my education, like Eliot House at breakfast, lunch, and dinner. W. J. Bate and resident tutors ate in the dining room. Argument and discussion continued while we ate, and the dining hall was a locus for the audacity of Harvard banter. I remember sliding my tray onto a table peopled by musicians—a flautist who studied musicology, an organist good enough to play on Harvard's Busch-Reisinger organ. Sitting down I announced, "Music is immoral," and we were off. Also there were girlfriends, there were dates. Marie took the train from New Haven for some weekends, staying at the Commander Hotel. Among the Harvards, whom she did not take to, she was silent. I began to understand that she did not belong to the nation in which I took citizenship. I loved her, she loved me, and I felt nauseated for a month over the notion of a breakup. One weekend in Connecticut, I ended our romance after three years. We wept and wept. I knew it was inevitable and felt heavy with sorrow and guilt. We parked for hours, not kissing but crying. As I drove home, a line of poetry floated into my head: "I walked all through you." In my bedroom I wrote many stanzas, guilty that I exploited our misery, unable to stop. Twelve lines remain, "Love Is Like Sounds"—the second-oldest poem I reprint in *White Apples and the Taste of Stone.*

A couple of months later, a friend of mine, with whom Marie and I had double-dated, broke up with his girl. I spent weekends hitchhiking to her college. She was pretty, sexy, and melodramatic: a pale, unsmiling face with black hair and red-red lipstick. My parents never mentioned her erotic demeanor, but she made them nervous. I was home one Christmas, preparing to return to Cambridge to see her for New Year's Eve, when she wrote a letter saying that she had her period, and she supposed I was *glad*—rebuking my presumed relief. One late afternoon I returned from an errand to find my mother agitated, smoking one cigarette after another, pacing. When my father's car pulled up to the curb, as he came home from work, my mother bolted out the door, slipped into the front seat beside him, and they drove off. I was bewildered. When they returned after a few minutes, my mother dashed upstairs, and my father, smiling with nervous false warmth, invited me into the den "for a heart-to-heart talk"—he used those very words—which of course plunged my heart into my penny loafers. In her anxiety over my girlfriend, my mother had snooped and read the letter. My father was controlling himself, as we sat in the den, and his attempts at a kindly smile turned his face into a gargoyle's. I explained that my girlfriend's worry was groundless; her pregnancy would have required a miracle. He believed me; then he said, matter-of-factly, that of course I could not return to Harvard, early, for New Year's Eve and my date. It was one of those moments. I said that I would indeed return for the date. He said I wouldn't, I said I would. He said that if I did, I was kicking my mother's body. In the end, they drove me to Cambridge and spent the night in a hotel, guilt-making through benignity. I dated my date and sleepily ate breakfast with my parents.

No one who loves poetry, and Cambridge, fails to praise the Grolier Poetry Book Shop. It was started in 1927 by Gordon Cairnie, later continued and improved by Louisa Solano. When I read Louise Bogan's *New Yorker* review of Wilbur's *The Beautiful Changes,* I crossed the street from the Harvard Yard to buy it at the Grolier. I dropped in every day, and there met Richard Eberhart and Richard Wilbur and Robert Creeley. (Fifty years later, it remained the first place I visited when I got to Cambridge.) It was tiny, with narrow volumes of poetry on shelves that almost reached the high ceiling; above the books were photographs of poets. In Gordon's day, he kept a lumpy green sofa where he sat smoking his pipe, his cronies beside him. He did not seem much interested in selling books. His wife Anna, he confided, owned stock in Atcheson, Topeka, and Santa Fe; it was Atcheson, Topeka, and Santa Fe that bankrolled the poetry bookstore. When I taught in Michigan, it was rare that I could come calling. The moment I walked in the door, Gordon would lock up and we would drink beer at the King's Tavern. When Gordon died and Louisa took over, she did not have the backing of a railroad. She increased stock, handled mail orders, sponsored readings, and instituted an annual Grolier Prize, publishing yearly a pamphlet of prizewinners.

Another unique institution was the Poetry Room, moved from Widener Library to Lamont while I was a student. Before the advent of the poetry reading, before tapes, it was startling to listen to poets reading their poems. Harvard's William Packard for years had sat down visiting poets before a machine that produced enormous 16-rpm records. Wearing earphones in the Poetry Room, I heard Dylan Thomas for the first time. I listened to the strange accents of Ezra Pound, who was now restricted to an insane asylum in Washington. In the Poetry Room were also copies of all poetry magazines, not so numerous then, and a lush library of contemporary work. Another locus was a writerly Harvard lunch club, the Signet. Editors of the *Crimson* ate there, as well as people from the *Lampoon* and the *Advocate*. My friendship with George Plimpton began at a Signet lunch. Bly and I ate there together. When you were elected to the Signet, you were required to address facetious remarks to the membership. I remember the title of John Ashbery's speech: "The Return of the Screw."

When Frank O'Hara was about to graduate, John and Judith Ciardi invited Frank and Ted Gorey and me to their house for spaghetti. It was a farewell party for Frank, and he was facing the graduate's familiar problem: "What will I *do?*" Ciardi had answers. "Get a scholarship to Michigan and win a Hopwood." (The popular 1920s playwright Avery Hopwood—*Getting Gertie's Garter*—left his fortune to the University of Michigan, income to be distributed to student writers.) At the supper table, Ciardi wrote Roy Cowden, who ran the Hopwood program, asking for a scholarship for Frank. Frank got the scholarship, won a Hopwood, and became Frank O'Hara. He wrote his wealth of poetry; he became a curator at the Museum of Modern Art; he was run over by a jeep on Fire Island and died.

After Ciardi's class, I had taken another creative writing course from Theodore Morrison. In this class I remember an epiphany about writing, when Morrison talked about the difference between a sketch and a story. I began to grasp notions of scale. I learned something similar the next year in Archibald MacLeish's class. Because I worked on poems for hours every day, I was offended when MacLeish called me lazy. He referred not to hours worked but to the ambition of my endeavor, to a conflict between apparent size and real scale. From MacLeish I learned lessons about *ear*, the poetic quality that MacLeish himself was best at, and from him I took the notion of a regular schedule. The writers he had known—he had a way of referring to "Scott, Ernest, and Dos"—worked every day at a regular hour. I took to hauling my typewriter after lunch to a tiny cubicle in the Lamont Library. It was a bad choice for the hour; after lunch I am comatose. In my last year at Harvard, I started the schedule I have followed ever since. I rose at six—the hour at which in New Hampshire my grandmother woke me with black coffee—and walked to the Square with folders and paper and pens. I drank black coffee, many cups, and worked on poems in the booth of an all-night cafeteria called Albiani's. At eight I walked back to Eliot House for breakfast.

While I remember Harvard as coming home—finding people like myself, making friendships that endured—I also remember depression. There were fights with friends, losses of affection and love, drunken idiocies, discouragement over classwork and, worse, the frequent conviction that I would never write a good poem. Migraine headaches continued from time to time, and I had come to know a doctor at the college health services who took an interest and gave me an electroencephalogram. (He said that my brain waves looked as if I had a family history of epilepsy.) I don't remember the circumstances, junior year, when I decided that I would quit school. On a miserable day I knew that I was breaking into fragments; I had to leave Harvard, I suppose returning to Ardmore Street and the ministrations of my mother. Sitting at my typewriter, I wrote the doctor a long letter telling him a hundred symptoms, with descriptions of anguish. When I finished pouring everything out, I felt immensely sleepy, and napped for two hours. When I woke I felt fine and tore up the letter.

One summer vacation, Robert Bly and I hitchhiked together down south. First he came to visit me at Ardmore Street. I dreaded his meeting my parents — my wild poet friend meeting my conventional mother and my father who was always anxious to please. What would Robert *say* to plunge me into embarrassment? Talk went innocently or fatuously at first. For Robert, it may have been his first experience of an eastern suburban middle-middle-class household. Robert was the son of a prosperous farmer, a Norwegian American from western Minnesota, and he had grown up working in the fields. He felt and enjoyed an alienation from the bland East he had invaded. At the table, he flirted with my mother as he did with all females. He ignored my father, who was quiet and nervous. Toward the end of the meal, he said, "Well, Mr. Hall, what do you think of having a son who's a poet?" My father twisted in agony. He recognized the challenge in the question. What could he say? I saved him, addressing my friend, "Too bad we can't ask your father the same thing." My father laughed eagerly, relieved by my "crack," as he would have called it.

My parents approved of our trip together, "as long as you don't hitchhike," which added disobedience to other pleasures. Hitchhiking, Bly and I carried provisions in Harvard book bags; I remember little tins of cocktail sausages. We took a bus to Virginia to commence our exploration. Walking in the woods at the end of the first day, we found a shelter with bunks, springs only, intended for provident hikers who carried sleeping bags. As we established ourselves, a small gang of Boy Scouts arrived. I remember the scoutmaster exclaiming at our book bags, "Is that your *gear*?" We slept ill. In the morning we found a road and hitchhiked ill. After seven or eight cars passed us, I hid in a ditch (two male hitchhikers are scarier than one) while Robert stepped out on the macadam, waving his arms, and forced a car to stop. I emerged from the side of the road, unshaven and unkempt. Robert explained to the driver that he and I had been chased by a bear and had fled from the woods to the road. Would he give us a lift? The driver was surely skeptical but unable to say no; Bly conned us a ride to the next town. There, we were so exhausted (the second night of our trip) that we rented a six-dollar room in a hotel and got some sleep. The next day we set out again, tired and grumpy. Short rides took us into Tennessee, as one of us hitched while the other napped in a ditch. I remember my fury when my friend decided not to take a turn with his thumb stuck out. Then an old man picked us up to drive us into a small town. When we arrived, I announced that I was going to take a bus back to Washington and go home. We didn't say much. Riding the Trailways, I realized with relief that the friendship had ended forever. Within weeks we were writing letters again, sending each other poems.

In the late forties there was much to-do about the revival of poetic drama. T. S. Eliot was the poet on the top of the mountain, and his verse plays stimulated the effort. There had been the *Fragment of an Agon*, and the pageant of *The Rock*, then *Murder in the Cathedral*, which was at least a poem for actors. *The Family Reunion* came closer to a play as the West End and Broadway knew plays, but not close enough. With *The Cocktail Party*, Eliot wrote something that filled seats, its success propelled partly by his Nobel Prize and partly by Alec Guinness. Eliot followed with more plays, well made in prosy lines. Then an Englishman named Christopher Fry wrote successful plays in verse, including *The Lady's Not for Burning*. Fry's plays are second rate, but for many people at the time they seemed to prove the return of poetic drama. At Harvard, some of us started the Poets' Theatre. We first gathered at Richard Eberhart's house in Cambridge, with Lyon Phelps as instigator of the meeting. Robert Bly was there, I think John Ashbery, maybe Frank O'Hara coming up from New York. We planned to produce plays, and daydreamed of our own space. In a few years, when I was back in Cambridge as a junior fellow, the Poets' Theatre had contrived a place of its own and a director.

In June of 1950, just after Robert Bly graduated, he and I drove in his green 1946 Buick to Bennington College in Vermont on a double blind date. I cannot remember who fixed us up; Bennington girls were rumored to be friendly. We drank beer with two pleasant young women at a tavern in upstate New York. We talked and told stories, laughed, kissed them goodnight, and slept in the car. In the morning, as we drove back to Cambridge, we learned from the car radio that North Korea had invaded the South, the United Nations was in session, war was about to begin. We hardly spoke of the war; we could hardly speak. As we were passing farms, Bly suddenly swerved the car to a stop beside a field of alfalfa. He wanted to walk in the field, and asked me to drive the car back by myself.

Henceforth, the war occupied the summer, and thoughts for the future. As a veteran, Robert was exempt from the draft. When I returned to college in September to begin my senior year, I received the expected letter, telling me to report to the New Haven Armory for a physical exam. Like everyone I knew, I did not want to be inducted. To avoid the peacetime draft, many of my classmates had earlier joined the Platoon Leaders Class of the Marines, and spent summers in training. They would be called up as second lieutenants when they graduated. (Six of my PLC classmates were dead in Korea within a year of graduation, one awarded a posthumous Congressional Medal of Honor.) I took the train to New Haven and showed up at the armory at the appointed hour and underwent the dreary process, naked lines undergoing stethoscopes and probing: "Cough." At the end, a Sergeant Piacek called us up, in groups of four or six, to hear the good news that we were classified 1-A and would be drafted. (The few 4-Fs didn't seem happy either.) With each group, the sergeant would slap one man on the shoulder and address a jocular remark. When my gang was called, Sergeant Piacek cheerfully assured me, "I'm going to make you my lead scout!"

In a few days, General Lewis Hershey, the director of the Selective Service System, announced student deferments. We would be able to graduate. Still, the war was the landscape of our senior year. A bunch of us improvised fake radio programs on a used wire recorder my father gave me at Christmas, making up a game show called "The Giant Broom." A cheerful MC (I took the part) interviewed a contestant who was invariably crippled or supporting a blind daughter or otherwise subject to pity and pathos, who was desperately in need of the million dollars, tax-free, available for a correct answer. When contestants failed—to compute the square root of negative one; to recite the Greek alphabet, backward, in nine seconds—they were swept by the Giant Broom into an incinerator where they sizzled in full view of a cheering studio audience. On the wire, a scream or two punctuated the applause.

In the spring of that year, the Poets' Theatre staged my one-act play *The Minstrel's Progress.* (I found a copy when I unpacked the boxes.) I wrote it largely in tetrameter couplets—Yeats and Marvell—and took my plot from a children's book by Eleanor Farjeon, *Martin Pippin in the Apple Orchard,* which I read on the recommendation of a girlfriend. It was a musical, songs sung by the leads: a girl (played by Harvey Lyon's wife) imprisoned by her jealous father (who ranted in Skeltonics), and a young man who courted her (played by an Exeter and Eliot House friend who years later became an assistant secretary of state). My friend the flautist wrote the music. He confessed later that he arrived at his melodies by tracing the contours of the New York skyline. *The Minstrel's Progress* played one night in 1951, and there has been no talk of a revival. I directed it and reserved for myself the small role of a wizard, who is employed by the father to exorcise the orchard; I incanted surreal, liturgical lines modeled on difficult passages from Hart Crane and Dylan Thomas. Archibald

MacLeish and Harry Levin sat in the front row. The play was brief—but its size exceeded its scale.

Otherwise, my senior year was an *annis mirabilis*. I won the annual poetry prize and another for a verse translation of Horace. I became president of the *Advocate* and was Class Odist at graduation. Most important, I was given a Henry fellowship to Oxford. The Henry sends two American students a year to Cambridge or Oxford, and two Englishmen a year to Harvard or Yale. Until my senior year, I had never thought of a fellowship overseas. When such a possibility occurred to me, it was too late to try for a Rhodes, but the Henry was still open. I applied and was interviewed. I remember one interlocutor asking if I thought it a good thing that *Time* had put T. S. Eliot on its cover. I answered that it was fine but that *Time* had shortly invalidated its judgment by putting Christopher Fry on its cover as well. I was asked if I was a snob about Fry, and I denounced Fry's work, quoting bad lines. Later that day I met a straight-A student from Honors English—Junior Eight Phi Beta Kappa—who had just been interviewed for a Henry. He asked me what we talked about, and I said, "Oh, I damned Christopher Fry." He looked surprised and said that Christopher Fry had come up in his interview also. I asked him what he had said, and he told me that he had characterized Fry as an immature talent who might perhaps over time develop into a playwright of importance . . . I was sure that interviewers would prefer his equivocation to my arrogance, but he did not become a Henry fellow. Chutzpah won the day, as it tends to.

The Party School

IF HARVARD HAD BEEN coming home, Oxford was going away. Middle-class Americans did not routinely pop across the ocean in 1951, when for the first time I sailed away from my country. The summer after graduation began with a seven-day voyage to France, much cheaper than the seventeen-hour airplane journey, on a ship called the *Homeland,* a hulk returned to civilian service after use as a troopship during the war. It carted young Americans—we were all rich Americans then—to an unknown Europe. The *Homeland* had a German crew and Italian stewards and flew a Panamanian flag. Launched forty or fifty years earlier as a Swedish liner, it was the equivalent in 1951 of a prewar Chevy junker. Because the floor was awash, only three men occupied our four-bunk tourist cabin; we needed the fourth bed to keep our suitcases out of the bilge. The voyage was a continual party, college students from everywhere drinking beer and dancing the polka. Landing in Le Havre, I fell instantly dumb. I had studied French and read French novels without strain, but I could not utter a word when I found myself in France. My first act in Paris was to buy the Gallimard volumes of *À la Recherche du Temps Perdu.* Prudently counting my change, I discovered that I had been overcharged by twenty dollars. In my ridiculous French, I drew the clerk's attention to the error of her arithmetic.

Three of us from Harvard and Radcliffe traveled together on

our first trip to Europe. One Radcliffe girl was my girlfriend—we later married—and the other her dormitory mate. We entrained to Italy and spent two weeks gawking at monuments. I spoke phrase-book Italian with a southern accent, having studied the melody at Hamden High among children of Calabrian immigrants. In Florence I puzzled a waiter by requesting pizza, which had not yet migrated north. We left Italy traveling back through the south of France, then crossed the channel for a train ride to Edinburgh and its nascent summer festival. In the compartment we discovered that the English were not cold and aloof—possibly because at the start of our journey we struggled to appear cold and aloof. We were invited to visit families in London, in Glasgow, in York. At the festival, we saw performances and paintings and took lunches in pubs. Returned to London, we explored the Festival of Britain, where I saw my first big Henry Moores, outdoor sculpture scaled to compete with the natural world. At summer's end, my companions returned to Radcliffe, and I had three weeks alone in London before attempting Oxford. I stayed in Bloomsbury at a minimal hotel near the British Museum and T. S. Eliot's Faber and Faber. I patronized a restaurant that served a three-course meal for three shillings and sixpence—fifty cents—and wandered through London's museums. Some nights I went to the theater, standing in line for seats astonishingly cheap. I took in *The Lyric Revue*, laughed at Peter Ustinov's *The Love of the Four Colonels*, and disliked Donald Wolfit's *Tamburlaine the Great* at the Old Vic; Wolfit played Tamburlaine as Mussolini. I visited great bookstores, notably Foyle's and the secondhand bookstores in its Charing Cross neighborhood. Drunk on low prices—a dollar for a new book of poems—I bought too many books. It was a friendly, shabby London, postwar, post-empire, post-power, an England that endured rationing still. The country was polite, brave, and monochrome, the nineteenth century gone to ruin, imperialism hanging from its shoulders like a moth-eaten cape. Colonial habits endured. When I bought a sweater, the clerk gave me my choice of "sky blue" or "nigger brown." There was a hamburger chain called Wimpy's, after the character in *Popeye*; burgers at Wimpy's tasted like English sausage, which was not a bad thing.

My Oxford residence had been chosen for me, Christ Church College, known as the House. Its dean was a Canadian who had been a Henry fellow and liked to collect Henry fellows. It was my good luck to reside there, instead of Balliol, which was full of bright Americans who hung out together. Among the hundreds of students at Christ Church, only eight or ten were American, so I found myself in an alien world—alien especially because the House was busy with Etonians, Harrovians, Wyckhamists, and survivors of other eminent public schools. They did not resemble either Harvard's meritocracy or its St. Grottlesexers who would sell stocks and bonds. Christ Church went in for gentry who, it seemed, would never sell anything.

The train from London arrived at the Oxford depot, and a cab deposited me at the entrance to the House, which was Christopher Wren's Tom Tower. Two gentlemen (as I saw them) wearing bowler hats approached the taxi, determined my identity, and seized my suitcases, heavy by courtesy of Foyle's. Each porter was of a certain age, and I protested that *I* should carry the suitcases—a social error of American naïveté that the tolerant porters had encountered before. I followed them through Tom Quad.

We passed a stone column holding up the entrance to the Hall, where shortly I would eat three appalling meals a day. We walked past Old Library, the eldest portion of the House, and came up against the House's newest structure, a Victorian row that fronted on Christ Church Meadows, and which contained my pair of rooms: Meadow Buildings 4/4. The porters led me upstairs, carrying my suitcases, to meet in my sitting room a small handsome fellow, a few years older than me, who undid me by his greeting: "Good morning, sir. I am your servant, sir."

He was my scout. With the help of a female bedder—bedmaking was women's work—Nobby Clark attended me and the rest of Meadow Buildings 4. Every morning he brought me a pitcher of hot water with which he filled a large china basin. There was no running water in my room, and no nearby bathroom. For one's morning toilette, the trick was never to let the hot water swish about and confuse one's deposits. Wash your hands and face using one area of water, brush your teeth using another, and shave using a third patch uncontaminated by the first two. Nobby would also supply coal for the fireplace in the sitting room; there was no source of heat in the bedroom. For a shilling or two he provided me with a waist-long academic gown, which I was required to wear when I left the college grounds. Later, when I bruised a knee—I staggered with a migraine and fell on the stones of Tom Quad—Nobby procured me a cane. Like all scouts, Nobby doubled as a waiter in Hall. His salary was minuscule, supplemented by tips from his masters. At the end of each term I gave him a few pounds. When I threw a sherry party for the Poetry Society, and Nobby supplied the glasses and cleaned up, I tipped him extra.

When I met him that first morning, I asked him to sit down. He demurred. Although we often talked in my room, he never sat in my presence. He had served five years in the British Army, North Africa through Italy into France. He was proud of his children, who would use the Butler Education Act to further their schooling, and who would never become scouts or bedders. Nobby himself had begun to work at Christ Church when he was fourteen, as a "scout's boy," which in his accent sounded like "scoot's buoy." While he unpacked for me, I wandered tentatively out to the street and found a pub: a pint of bitter and two sausages for lunch. I walked through Carfax to Broad Street where I discovered Blackwell's, as splendid as Foyle's. Used books were shelved alongside new. (I found a first edition of Ezra Pound's anthology *Des Imagistes*, 1912, for seven shillings, or a dollar.) I walked on wide streets and narrow, past old buildings that were clearly colleges, past tearooms and an establishment called Ducker & Son that made bespoke shoes, past pubs and restaurants. I wandered into the deer park at Magdalene. I encountered swans. Speaking to no one, I succumbed to the glorious golden dazzle of that October afternoon. Walking back toward my rooms, I looked through the House's quadrangles. Scaffolding rose in front of the library, where workmen were busy restoring the rotten stone of the façade. A sign advised us to stay clear of falling chunks. Nearby was Peckwater Quad, later I learned the noblest quarters, which contained a boy with red hair who was Christ Church's only resident earl. When someone in London asked your college, Christ Church students tended to reply, "I'm up at the House." The most elevated could say they were "up at Peck."

Just past Meadow Buildings I found the Fellows' Garden, enclosed behind a stone wall with gate ajar. Inside, autumn flowers bordered a flat greensward, rolled for centuries, where students played bowls. All year the college's gardeners and groundskeepers unobtrusively tended this secret, silent place. Through a portal midway down Meadow Buildings, I entered Christ Church Meadows, acres of countryside walled away from the crowded city. Cows grazed the Meadows, and solitary walkers, or friends in pairs, made use of the wide paths. My sitting room's tall windows fronted the Meadows. The room contained a large table at which I would work, an old fireplace narrowed by new bricks to save fuel, three chairs, and a battered Victorian sofa. Meadow Buildings was erected long before austerity; I imagined great blazing coal fires tended by a scout. That night I had my first dinner in Hall, sparsely populated because term had not begun, a desperate meal of rabbit diced with bones, overcooked vegetables, and soggy potatoes. On the walls were portraits of distinguished folk associated with the House, including Holbeins of Henry VIII and his daughter Elizabeth, and an oil of Cardinal Wolsey, who had founded the House. (King Henry finished the establishment after he finished the cardinal.) A more recent portrait showed C. L. Dodgson, Alice's maker, who had been a Christ Church don of mathematics.

This great rich high dazzling room was lonely not only because few students had returned but because no one spoke to me. In days to come, when the Hall filled with young men, it became lonelier. All communication employed the tones of irony. If I asked someone to pass the salt, I revealed my provenance by my accent, and heard in response something that sounded rude. Feeling snubbed at every meal, I avoided asking for salt. Eventually I learned the language, and discovered that rudeness was a mating call. If you responded to rudeness with rudeness, you might begin a friendship. At Harvard the style had differed, although we also managed to be rude: In the furnace of discussion, we insulted each other by accusations of feeble intelligence. Such an insult at Oxford would appear pretentious. The House's rudeness was light, *lightly* insulting, and nothing should seem heavy or serious. To talk with enthusiasm was to be a dork; to display intelligence was ostentatious and violated the social code. After six weeks, I had acquired a tone of frivolity. Other Americans in the House, who had survived a year or two of Oxford, gave me counseling.

Oxford published two weekly magazines, the *Isis* and the *Cherwell*, edited by students for students. Each featured a gossip column, where the same names of eminent undergraduates turned up week after week. Some eminence was social, people with titles of nobility, but eminence was also accorded actors and poets. Notorious were the leads in productions of the Oxford University Dramatic Society (OUDS) and poets who published in *Isis*. It surprised me that poetry could be a tool of celebrity. In November I sent two poems to *Isis*, Wilburish things. I heard nothing, but in a week both turned up in print—and I received invitations to parties. The first Saturday after publication I went to a party in somebody's digs, where the literati of Oxford drank sherry. I arrived with a cane, after my fall in Tom Quad, and found myself installed in a chair with a footstool. One after one, vertical guests paid me visits. I remember a question from a handsome undergraduate woman who was engaged to marry an Oxford poet: "Do you need that cane or is it affectation?" I was invited to BYOB parties, sherry parties, gin fests. Before long I had met everyone who was writing at Oxford. Oxford was a party school.

England at this time, when it encountered Americans, combined good feeling with envy and condescension. The English saw themselves as more civilized, more sophisticated, more subtle—but also decadent, a collapsing empire of power and art. Americans were energetic, slow-witted, rich, generous, vulgar, and victorious. (It resembles the way the French have seen themselves against the English.) My nationality even frightened people; one Oxford poet confessed to me that I had been scary because I talked American and wore tennis shoes. Of course I exploited my perceived vitality among the exhausted gentry of imperialism. I presented myself as the professional poet, the technician. At the *Advocate*—I told everyone at Oxford—we argued about images and line breaks; at Oxford, despite its predilection for frivolity, no one spoke of poems as made things. An Oxford poet, who later became a friend and an advertising mogul, criticized me for including in a poem a reference to something contemporary—Marks and Spencer? World War II? He told me that poetry should be pure and timeless; you should never use words that would require a footnote in a hundred years. I answered by quoting Chaucer on the cook: "Many a Jack of Dover hath he sold / That hath been twice hot and twice cold." (A Jack of Dover was a meat pie, and if it did not sell one day, the cook withdrew the gravy, to reinject it heated up another day—with predictable results to the medieval gastric system.) I claimed that "Jack of Dover" was more poetry than "congestible foodstuff."

At Oxford, poetry was an attitude, not an art. It annoyed me to find, in the country of poetry, poetry degraded by prohibitions against taking anything seriously. One eminent London poet called poetry "a modest art." Among my fellow students virtually no one took poetry the way we took it on the *Advocate*, as art to make, to work at as a sculptor works at stone. Many people repeated the saw "To be a poet at twenty is to be twenty; to be a poet at thirty is to be a poet." The critic Christopher Ricks came up after me, and heard tales. When I met him decades later, he asked me if it was true that I had said—he adopted an Al Capone accent—"Ya gotta fake it, but ya gotta fake it good." Probably I did. One Oxford poet composed a Clerihew:

> Donald Hall
> Is fat and tall
> But the ego within the matter
> Is taller and fatter.

Because I expressed my irritation with Oxford poetry, people feared me and I found myself deferred to. I was appointed literary editor of the *Isis*, and secretary of OUPS, which meant I would preside over the Poetry Society the following term. I would invite poets from the larger world to read us their poems, which they did for expenses only. I entertained Louis MacNeice, Vernon Watkins, Kathleen Raine, W. R. Rogers, C. Day-Lewis, Dylan Thomas.

My Oxford was the university more than the House. In the social mores of Oxford, one could be active within one's college or one could put oneself forward in the university at large—but if one was English, one could not do both. It was acceptable to take part in activities within the House's walls—clubs for theater or beagling or rowing or politicking—but it was unseemly to be known in the larger university world, OUDS in theater or *Isis* in literature. Because my poems and my name turned up in *Isis*, I would have been *infra dig* in the House if I had been a normal undergraduate. I could get away with it because it was understood that Americans didn't know any better.

And I made friends who have remained friends over the decades, mostly from the less social schools and even from grammar schools not private but public. There was the poet George Mac-Beth, who succeeded me as president of the Poetry Society and who became a talks producer at the BBC, for whom I made frequent broadcasts. He visited me in Ann Arbor and in New Hampshire. Robin Jordan I knew in the House, a talented actor who despised acting. We played squash racquets together and stayed up late, talking and drinking Nescaf, as everybody called it. One spring day he took me with him to visit his old school, Charterhouse. He introduced me to masters and walked me through his old precincts on a bright English day in June. An Oxford college was playing cricket at Charterhouse that day, and we rode home on the cricketers' bus (we had journeyed by train), which stopped for two hours at a country pub. Alastair Elliot was also in the House, a poet straight out of school, naïve and intense, and dedicated to poetry although dedication was prohibited. We stay in touch, and have visited each other in England and America. Jenny Joseph and Elizabeth Jennings were poets I saw much of, and Jenny visited me in Paris and later in New Hampshire. My closest friend was Geoffrey Hill, whom I met at the end of my first year. He had published a poem in *Isis* that I admired, and I invited him to my rooms for a Poetry Society sherry party. When I praised his poem, he reacted with an effusion of gratitude that I took as ironic. I was overprepared for mockery, and my reaction was mistaken. Geoffrey came from a village where his father was constable, and he had been educated in state schools before winning a scholarship to Keble. For him at that time, a Poetry Society sherry party in Christ Church was an audience with the Queen. I invited him to submit poems for the Fantasy Poets pamphlet series.

Published by a painter who owned a manual printing press, and edited by the OUPS president, the Fantasy Poets had started earlier that term with four poetry pamphlets, of which mine was the last. Now that I was incoming president of the Poetry Society, I would edit the next series. That summer, when I was back briefly in New Hampshire, Hill mailed me his manuscript. I read "Genesis" and other extraordinary poems written by a twenty-year-old from a Worcestershire village. I woke in the middle of the night to turn on the light and read the poems again, they were so shockingly good. The next year at Oxford I saw Hill almost every day. He had grown up reading an Oscar Williams anthology, and unlike others at Oxford knew contemporary American poetry and favored it. He was impressed that I actually knew Richard Eberhart. We talked poetry in our digs and at pubs and on walks; we talked Robert Lowell and Theodore Roethke and Richard Wilbur. For his twenty-first birthday, I drove him to his village for lunch with his parents. (My Morris Minor was a wedding present. In the summer between my two Oxford years, I returned to the United States and married my Radcliffe sweetheart; she spent the next year with me in Oxford.) In the decades after Oxford, I saw Geoffrey when I returned to England, and after Jane and I moved to New Hampshire he took to visiting us at the farm, flying from England in the summer, until he settled teaching in Boston.

Thom Gunn was an undergraduate at Cambridge, and Oxford heard his poems broadcast on a Third Programme literary magazine called *New Soundings*. In England in those years, if you identified a dangerous rival, you asked him to your club. We invited Gunn to come over from Cambridge, and we threw a party to welcome him. A couple of weeks later I visited Cambridge, where Thom walked me around the colleges and introduced me to friends. When I returned to the United States, we wrote letters, sending each other poems, talking about poetry in our two countries, talking about prosody. I spent that year at Stanford on a fellowship, studying with Yvor Winters. Thom was eager to get to the United States. I encouraged him to apply for the Stanford fellowship, and when he tried, I argued for him with Winters. Thom took up the fellowship the next year, and discovered California, where he spent most of his life.

Oxford's party was continuous. Christ Church closed its gate at a quarter past midnight. If one was detained by the urgencies of a BYOB party, one had to struggle over a wall for late entry. I fell into a drainage ditch trying to climb into the Meadows. Two constables rescued me and woke up the night porter: "This man says 'is name is Donald 'all." "So 'e is. So 'e is." When I came to breakfast the next morning, scouts giggled behind their hands. Not all social occasions were so boisterous. Within the House, I was elected to a facetious debating society, the Twenty Club. We were nineteen students. The twentieth was our senior member, the oldest goldfish in Tom Quad's Mercury Pool. He attended only the annual meeting, brought by a member in a waterproof cardboard box. When he was introduced there were cries of "impostor" as other members raised aloft their own goldfish in cardboard boxes. If resolutions for debate seemed ribald, the trick was to change them into something boring and high-minded. If the topics appeared sober, the task was to make them ribald. Canon Jenkins was a venerable Augustinian scholar in Christ Church. The Twenty Club invited him as a guest to debate the proposition "Resolved: That cannons without cannon-balls are an abomination." In his creaking voice the canon declined: "I think . . . I detect . . . a duplicity."

My Oxford was an old, waning Oxford, the institution of Waugh's *Brideshead Revisited* become shabbier but still exquisite. One literary undergraduate indeed carried a teddy bear everywhere he went; it was rumored that he was secretly heterosexual. Other undergraduates lived out plots that reminded me of Victorian romances. There was the vicar's son who fell in love with a glorious trollop, who was good-natured, beautiful, lower class, and expensive. Somehow he contrived to borrow money, for jewels and finery, which he could never hope to repay. He ended up in old-style imperial exile, poor in a postcolonial West Indian town, clerking and bookkeeping among lizards and beetles. And there was an undergraduate called Nigel who gave Stilton parties every Sunday noon, with bottles of South African sherry to go with the cheese. It was impossible to buy Stilton in Oxford at the time—I survived on Danish blue—because Stilton was reserved for export, to help with the kingdom's balance of payments. But Nigel had an illicit source, so that in pursuit of Stilton, Oxford's most notorious types came to his rooms at noon every Sunday: lords and ladies, actors and poets, the prettiest and most powerful undergraduates. Unfailingly, Nigel's parties were noticed in the gossip columns of *Isis* and *Cherwell*, whose editors unfailingly attended. It was known that Nigel did not come from money, and we wondered how he managed. It turned out that Nigel also incurred massive debts. He did not follow the vicar's son into exile but took another route. He sold to one of England's tabloids his tales of a dope-crazed Oxford, featuring drunken sex orgies. He cleared his debts and was never seen again.

Vacations, I flew to Paris, also shabby but its food gorgeous and abundant. Dinner cost a dollar, and made up for Hall, or for Oxford restaurants like the Café de Paris, which we pronounced "caif duh Parris." We were eating in the caif when a Canadian, just back from France, ordered its choucroute garnie, assured by the Indian waiter that it was the real thing. In Paris I occasionally afforded the real thing at the Brasserie Lipp: an Alsatian dish of pork or ham, sausage, and sauerkraut. When the Oxford version arrived, it was a scoop of canned sauerkraut, an English sausage, and a great mound of undercooked chips. At only one restaurant in Oxford could one taste anything, an Indian restaurant inevitably called the Taj Mahal. A year before my arrival, the establishment had been fined for selling cat and calling it beef. Its menu now listed "meat." I usually ate keema matar, cat or not, but I was once taken for lunch by a friend from the House who had grown up in India, scion of generations of a Scottish merchant family in Bengal. Hamish Murray asked, "May I order for you?" I took one bite and burst into flames. Hamish signaled to the waiter. "Bring this man a dish of ice cream."

So far, I have omitted disclosure of my academic duties, which has not been difficult. In my two years, I did not attend a lecture. Oxford was a place where I wrote poems, went to parties, and carried on about poetry. Once a term I was invited to pay a call on my moral tutor, a Christ Church don who formed my official connection to the college. He was J.I.M. Stewart, a critic and scholar who was better known as a writer of detective stories under the name of Michael Innes. When I drank my termly glass of sherry with him, he was pleasant enough but often pricked me with reference to my nationality. It was a B.Litt. that I read for, a two-year degree for which there is no American equivalent. I needed to turn in a paper—maybe a hundred pages—at the end of the second year. Midway through the first year there were exams to take, which accomplished little except to prove that one was intent on taking a B.Litt. One three-hour paper examined us on Locke, Berkeley, and Hume. The other paper was preparatory to scholarship, and related to a literary period. B.Litt. candidates studied "Sources, Methods, and Authorities" for one era. Since I expected eventually to write about modern literature, I chose the latest period offered, which was Victorian. I crammed. I read a book on the history of the Macmillan Company, psyching out a question on publishing, and at my viva, or oral examination, I was congratulated, not without irony, on my erudition about the Macmillan Company. In the philosophy viva, I received a mild rebuke. I had referred to Samuel Johnson's refutation of Berkeley's idealism: He kicked a stone to prove Berkeley wrong. My philosophical examiner objected that I had characterized Johnson as an intelligent man.

For my thesis I wanted to write about prosody, intending in years hence to investigate the prosody of modernist poetry. Normally a supervisor would come from my college, but only one

don at Oxford had any interest in the subject, a woman named
Catherine Ing, attached to St. Hilda's. We met, talked about a
suitable topic, and came up with the subject of prosodists—people who write about the sound and meter of English verse—in the
eighteenth century. Thus when I returned to Oxford my second
autumn, I read decaying volumes in Oxford's Duke Humphrey
Library, the oldest part of the Bodleian, and traveled to London
for the British Museum when the Bodley lacked a book. From the
first notes to the final paper took sixteen weeks. I became the author of "Eighteenth Century Prosodists, with Especial Attention to Edward Bysshe and Joshua Steele."

In the spring of my first year, I took Oxford's annual prize for
a poem, the Newdigate Prize, previously won by Matthew Arnold,
Oscar Wilde, and a few other recognizable names. (Because the
prize is annual, the list of winners is not impressive.) Announcement of the forthcoming competition had appeared in the autumn, posters all over Oxford. The title for the poem is supplied,
and this year it was "Exile"—an existential topic, enhanced by a
century of political persecution. The word allowed me shame-
lessly to exploit my distance from my native land. My pseudo-
nym for the anonymous competition, lest anyone should miss
the point, was "E. Pluribus-Unum." When I saw the announcement, I knew that I would enter the competition, although the
final sentence on the poster was discouraging: "The poem need
not be written in heroic couplets." I wrote "Exile" in Paris. During Christmas and Easter holidays, each six weeks long, I lived
on the fifth floor of the small Hôtel du Pavillon on the Left Bank.
Each morning *la petite bonne* brought me a croissant and black
coffee—black coffee at breakfast, a scandal in France—and I lay

in bed writing "Exile" until noon. The rest of the day I thought
about dinner. For lunch I ate a ham or cheese sandwich in a café,
then looked at paintings in museums, then ate a gorgeous meal
for a dollar at Raffi or the Restaurant des Beaux Arts. Occasionally I spent a dollar and a half to eat at Le Petit Saint-Benoît.
Sometimes in the evening I heard music—American folksingers
at L'Abbaye, Sidney Bechet's jazz at the Vieux-Colombier. The
great New Orleans musician then lived in Paris at the Montana, a
hotel on rue Saint-Benoît. Afternoons he sat in front of his hotel
on a kitchen chair tilted back, and I took pains to walk past him
almost daily, saying, "Good afternoon, Mr. Bechet." "Good afternoon," he would reply. I ended the night drinking Alsatian beer,
"la bonne pain d'Alsace," at Brasserie Lipp with other American
graduates in Europe.

Newdigate submissions were due as the third term began,
and late in the term I learned that I had won. C. Day-Lewis,
who was a judge, came to my rooms to propose revisions. H. R.
Trevor-Roper wrote me that he had regretted not fining me for
my "recent adventures" in the drainage ditch—the author of
The Last Days of Hitler was at the moment Senior Censor of
Christ Church—but that he no longer felt regret. Reporters interviewed me, and I was subject to much attention. One of the
conditions of the prize was that the poet should read from the
poem at a university ceremony called Encaenia at the end of
term. I read a few stanzas, in what the *Times* called "a suitably
lugubrious voice." Recently an American had been for the first
time elected to lead the Oxford Union, the university's debating
society, which served as a nursery for parliamentarians, and another American had won the Chancellor's English Essay Prize.

English newspapers spoke of Yanks taking over Oxford, and *Time* did a story on us, with our photographs.

Eventually, a side effect of "Exile" was my connection with the *Paris Review*. George Plimpton, whom I had known at Harvard, was enjoying Cambridge, and came over to play tennis, his King's College against my Christ Church. We had a bibulous dinner afterward, and he recruited "Exile" for the first issue of a new magazine starting in Paris. He asked me if I could find other poets for that issue; I supplied him with Robert Bly and others. Before the second issue appeared, I had become its poetry editor, and continued to choose its poems for ten years. I read through great stacks of manuscript during my last Oxford year, then at Stanford for a year, then back at Harvard on a fellowship, and in Ann Arbor when I first taught there. In my twenties, opinionated and passionate about new poetry, I found it gratifying to impose my taste on the world. The writers were largely American, but also I published young English poets: Thom Gunn and Geoffrey Hill at first, later Ted Hughes and Philip Larkin. I looked for unknown poets of my generation, reading other magazines with a greedy eye. One afternoon I wrote letters soliciting work from James Wright and Louis Simpson, whom I had been admiring from a distance. Both submitted good poems — and two friendships began. My acquaintance with George Plimpton endured for fifty years; I stayed in his apartment, visiting New York; I attended his riotous parties — where Artie Shaw and Peter Duchin competed to play the piano, where the skinny black guy was James Baldwin and the big one Archie Moore.

I was twenty-four years old in 1953 and the Newdigate brought me the poetic notice I had been seeking for ten years. Oscar Williams reprinted "Exile" in a drugstore paperback anthology. For years the Newdigate gave me an identity, which like most identities became irritating. "Exile" is a public poem, something to be read from a platform, written in an oratorical voice, and it became a decaying albatross that hung around my neck. I kept revising it, from printing to printing, trying to get it right or at least better. In 1968, when I did my first selected poems, I cut my hundred-line poem to eight lines.

Winning the Newdigate in 1953 had another, major impact on my life. The Korean War continued, and my student exemption from the draft had endured, but at about the time I won the prize, General Hershey of the Selective Service changed the rules. It turned out that rich Americans were enrolling at the Sorbonne, getting a leftist or pacifist professor to vouch for them, and dodging the draft in the guise of students, without actually studying. Hershey announced that henceforth only Rhodes Scholars and Fulbrights would be deferred for study abroad; therefore I would be drafted. Without consulting me, my father took *Time* with its story and photograph to the Selective Service appeal board in New Haven, and they exempted me. "Exile" and *Time* saved me from the Inchon Peninsula.

Toward the end of my second year, the Institute for Contemporary Arts, in London, put on an evening of discussion about Ezra Pound, the anti-Semite, still held captive in Washington at St. Elizabeths. He had broadcast to American troops during the war as an admirer of Mussolini and Italian fascism. T. S. Eliot spoke, and J. Isaacs, who was a critic and a Jew; Pound's anti-Semitism had been virulent. I read a Canto aloud, recruited for my American accent. The proceedings were intelligent and serious, subject only to one moment of levity or perhaps mayhem: Graham Greene and John Davenport entered the room, drunk and noisy, to demand that we cease our praise of the fascist. Thus I was in attendance at an occasion where a famous novelist, with his literary critic friend, was expelled from the room.

The next year I spent in California, as far from Oxford as I was likely to get. Pleasure in England and my English friends remained, and during the early years of my teaching, I returned to England twice for a year's leave. After Jane and I moved to Eagle Pond, in 1975, rural New Hampshire displaced my desire to spend time in England. We flew there for brief visits only. In 1981 I traveled alone from New Hampshire to Oxford to attend a Christ Church reunion, called a gaudy—from *gaudeo*, "I rejoice," as in *"Gaudeamus igitur"*; or as in Dorothy Sayers's *Gaudy Night*. I arrived with a full beard, fifty pounds heavier than I had been at the House. No one recognized me; I recognized no one. In Tom Quad we were served sherry and I stood miserably alone, or wandered among groups looking for a familiar face. Then someone spoke my name, and repeated his own, and memory bestirred itself. When we sat again reunited in Hall, the food was better, wine was abundant, and Sir Harold Macmillan delivered a droll after-dinner speech. We moved on to Founder's Port, an agreeable grape that pretended to have been put down by Cardinal Wolsey in the sixteenth century. Much Port, much Port. Much memory of much acquaintance, and a happy, blurry gaudy-return to the party school.

Coffee with Robert Graves

NOW I MUST TELL ABOUT times after Oxford and before my return to New Hampshire, but there's something large that I must
leave out. I will speak little of my first marriage. My wife and I had
two children, who have produced five grandchildren. The marriage ended after fifteen years—separation in 1967, divorce in
1969. As with all divorces, it derived from misery and produced
further misery. I missed my children and felt guilty about leaving them—although I was able to see them twice a week. Within
the marriage there had been adventure and happiness, especially
at the beginning and with the births of the children. Over the
Christmas break at Oxford, 1952–53, we drove our Morris Minor
convertible to France, through Germany to Vienna and out the
Soviet zone of Austria to Yugoslavia, then down to Greece, where
we spent two weeks in Athens. South of Belgrade, there were no
roads in Yugoslavia. When we got stuck in a muddy field, following a cart track, we were pulled out by helpful people passing by.
Reaching the last Yugoslav city before Greece, we were told that
our route had been unpassable. We agreed. The Marshall Plan
restored roads at the Greek border.

The last months at Oxford were devoted to what would happen
next. I had been admitted to study for a Ph.D. at Harvard. Long
before, I had decided to become a teacher to support my poetry
habit—but for now I wanted only to write. A friend at Oxford

told me about a yearlong creative writing fellowship at Stanford University, so I wound up translated from Banbury Road in Oxford to a pair of rooms in Menlo Park, California. I worked for a year with Yvor Winters, and my son Andrew was born in Stanford Hospital. I wrote "My Son My Executioner," which appeared in *The New Yorker*, and began to publish poems widely. For a few years at least I inflated with self-satisfaction. One friend told me that my letters sounded like press releases. I look back at an obnoxious young man, eager in pursuit of honor and fame. I wrote somewhere that the poet at fifteen wants to be as great as Dante; by twenty-five he wants to be in *The New Yorker*. I know where I got this notion.

While at Stanford, I was readmitted to Harvard graduate school—and avoided graduate school again by being elected to the Society of Fellows at Harvard. This position bore the burden of liberty: three years devoted to one's work—no teaching and no classroom study. For me the work was poetry. The Society of Fellows was founded in 1933 by the president of Harvard, Abbott Lawrence Lowell, who anonymously donated his own fortune, attempting with the society to provide an alternative to the Ph.D. Lowell deplored the omnipresence of the Teutonic doctorate in the academy. Many professors at an old Harvard had gone without graduate school—gentlemen eschewed professionalism—but now hoi polloi were writing dissertations, publishing books, and getting tenure. In Lowell's society, a group of senior fellows, mostly Harvard faculty, elected men in their mid-twenties, maybe seven a year, students of all disciplines and subjects. Junior fellows received a stipend during their tenure, with offices and labs and equipment as required. We worked on our own, without supervisors, sometimes inventing new fields of study. By the 1950s, the Society of Fellows no longer acted principally as a substitute for the Ph.D. Young scholars and scientists were frequently chosen after finishing course work toward a doctorate, and over their fellowship years conducted experiments, researched, and wrote books which served as dissertations. A poet, elected to write poems, was an exception. I excused myself happily from a doctorate. Poets had never been junior fellows until Richard Wilbur in 1947. He was a fellow when I was an undergraduate. Seven years older than me, a veteran of Anzio and France, he was generous to swap manuscripts with a nineteen-year-old. In 1954, John Hollander and I were elected, and for three years talked poetry, read each other's poems, and cheerfully rivaled each other.

On Monday nights the fellows congregated for sherry and dinner, seniors and juniors with their guests—an American High Table modeled on Oxford and Cambridge. We came from physics and history and mathematics and comparative religion and musicology and logic and economics and everything else. Edmund Wilson was a guest twice a year, T. S. Eliot every spring; once I had dinner with Vladimir Nabokov. Many eminent guests were scientists. At twenty-five, over sherry, I introduced one Nobel laureate to another—a physicist senior fellow, Ed Purcell, to Linus Pauling, the visiting chemist I had just met. The junior fellows themselves were notable, and accomplishing original work. The first Monday, I sat next to a saturnine young fellow who lacked small talk. I asked him what he was in. "Mathematical linguistics," he said. I told him I had not heard of the discipline, having just met Noam Chomsky.

These occasions could be antic. Sometimes the excitement was so great that on Monday nights after a dinner, I had trouble sleeping. Junior fellows determined the menus, and the chef encouraged us to be demanding. John Hollander constructed an evening beginning with an hors d'oeuvre of Wiener schnitzel à la Holstein. Abundant wine ascended from our cellars. After dessert, a wheeled funicular traveled the U-shaped table carrying Port and Madeira as we passed around a box of cigars. Renato Poggioli was a senior fellow and professor of comparative literature who didn't smoke cigars. I did. Every Monday, Renato picked his cigar from the box and threw it across the table in my direction, occasionally bopping a distinguished head.

Talk continued until late in the night. Marvin Minsky, a junior fellow who was inventing artificial intelligence, walked from one group to another, listening in and contributing a word or two before moving on. "Wittgenstein," he might say, dismissively. Conversation was acute and competitive. These young and older men—it would be decades before the society admitted women—were combative sorts, and all of them ate the world for starters. I enjoyed eavesdropping on alien shoptalk. Physicists sat together speaking of meson particles, apparently a problem of the moment. "This thing about meson particles," said one, "it won't *break*, it'll just *sag!*" Loud, mysterious laughter.

Every day I read literature and worked on poems, wrote book reviews and essays on poetry. I was living the life I had dreamed of. I baby-sat my infant son each morning while his mother finished her B.A. Adrienne Rich visited the apartment once a week, nine A.M. to one, to talk poetry while I fed Andrew breakfast, scraped oatmeal off the ceiling, changed his diapers, gave him a bath, set him down for a morning nap, and fed him lunch. Adrienne and I had become close friends during my second year at Oxford, where she chose to spend a Guggenheim year. Now we were back in Cambridge, and Adrienne was pregnant with her first child. She watched me sling Andrew over my shoulder like a book bag. Decades later, when I was divorced and Adrienne widowed, she visited me in Ann Arbor. I wondered aloud how chauvinist I had been in the fifties. "Don," she told me, "you taught me how to bathe a baby."

In May of 1955, my first Society of Fellows year, my father underwent exploratory surgery that disclosed an inoperable cancer. He was fifty-one. On the day the surgeon told us he would die, I received a letter from the Viking Press: It accepted my first book of poems, *Exiles and Marriages.* For the next seven months my father was dying as my first book progressed from copyedit to printed volume. Everything that I did, toward publication, felt interconnected with my father's death. I drove to Connecticut to see him once a week, showing him galley and pages. The progress of *Exiles* distracted him, and in October so did baseball, when we watched television while our Brooklyn Dodgers took a flickering seven-game World Series triumph over the Yankees. *Exiles and Marriages* came out early in December, and he held it in his hand. There were good reviews; negative ones didn't start until after his death. Early in December, *Time* praised *Exiles* in its lead review, with a photograph. My father devoted himself to *Time* every week, and I read him aloud the review. His voice was failing but he stammered out, "My cup . . . runneth . . . over." He died on December 22, 1955, and we buried him on Christmas Eve.

Exiles and Marriages was long and thin, not a good book, but it came out when literary journalism was looking for a new young poet, and I was chosen. The volume won a first-book prize and was nominated for the National Book Award. *Exiles* was formal, mostly written in rhymed stanzas or blank verse, coming out of a heyday of stanzas. Our immediate elders, like Allen Tate and John Crowe Ransom, had fought off the powerful modernist fathers by replicating seventeenth-century forms. Younger formalists followed, led by Karl Shapiro, then Robert Lowell and Richard Wilbur. Early in my teens I had written free verse — as I have done most of my life — but when I was seventeen I fell in love with meter and rhyme. I remember sitting at my table at the farm that summer, listening to my own pentameters, counting syllables and stresses, teaching myself the manners of meter. I became obsessed with its tricks and wonders, to the exclusion of other poetic elements. With my immersion in form, I found myself writing a *kind* of poem. It wasn't meter's fault; metrical poems can go anywhere and do anything. For me, these forms came to imply a reasonable poem. It sounds crazy now, but at that time I needed to understand what the poem was going to say before I began it. The better poems I wrote in my twenties — like "My Son My Executioner" and "The Sleeping Giant" — concealed a content I was not aware of. Most of my poems were impersonal and oracular even when they claimed the first person.

As I was finishing the late poems of *Exiles*, something in me began to feel stifled, dumb, inarticulate. My grand language failed to express or reveal crucial areas of feeling. I flailed about, looking for other ways to make a noise. I had admired Marianne Moore's syllabics — keeping a syllable count, avoiding metrical feet. Holding on to the count of syllables as to a guardrail, I wrote a poem called "Je Suis Une Table." I thought it was a poem of wit exploiting a language error—tables can't talk—but it wasn't; it was an outcry, complaining of habitual limitation or inhibition. This poem began a journey. Eventually, I no longer demanded that my poems explain themselves before they got written; I learned to trust the impetus, to ride the wave. The wave was feeling, expressed largely in long vowels. I worked by accepting an image compelled by rhythm and sound—without requiring that it explain its purpose.

Meanwhile, the poetry of my time was changing—and I resisted change even as my own poems began to change. After *Exiles and Marriages* I participated in an anthology—*The New Poets of England and America* (the *The* was remarked upon)—which I coedited with Robert Pack and Louis Simpson. It came out in 1957, pretty much 343 pages of verse that resembled *Exiles and Marriages*—witty, reasonable, and public. It included Lowell, Wilbur, Rich, Nemerov—the best we knew of its moment. Our collection was the first shot fired in the Battle of the Anthologies. We became known as the ACADEMIC POETS. Donald Allen's *New American Poetry* (1960) followed, embodying the BEAT GENERATION —small caps required. It was a celebrated conflict, but at the time of editing, Simpson and Pack and I weren't firing on Fort Sumter because we didn't know that Fort Sumter existed. We had never heard of Philip Whalen or Michael McClure—but it needs to be said that if we had read them, we would not have printed them. A year after *Exiles and Marriages* appeared, Allen Ginsberg read *Howl* at the Six Gallery in San Francisco, public birth of the Beat Generation—which shortly took over the world.

Forty years after *Howl*, I took part in a symposium the day Allen Ginsberg died. The younger panelists spoke of the liberation they felt when *Howl* appeared. Not me. As I confessed that day, when *Howl* came out I felt attacked, not liberated—my castle razed by barbarian hordes—and for a couple of years I denounced the Beats. I rejected Ginsberg's "Sunflower Sutra" for the *Paris Review*—whereupon Ginsberg told George Plimpton that I wouldn't know a poem if it buggered me in broad daylight. In editing and grumbling, I was defensive and conservative, ungenerous and conventional. I came around gradually, first by way of Black Mountain: Robert Creeley, Denise Levertov, Robert Duncan. I found Gary Snyder and his master Kenneth Rexroth. I praised Charles Olson's first *Maximus* in a *Nation* review. For a time, the Battle of the Anthologies raged among followers while the poets themselves turned ecumenical, departing the barricades to argue poetry while drinking beer. When I later introduced Ginsberg at an Ann Arbor reading, he told the audience that we had once been "the most famous enemies in the poetry world." He added, "And now we kiss each other."

I had been a famous enemy—a reactionary general, a leader of the White Guard—and movements need enemies. The battle always had its artificiality. The poets of Donald Allen's *New American Poetry* did not hang together by an ethos or an aesthetic—they differed greatly, although most wrote free verse—but all shared the characteristic that they had not been collected in *The New Poets of England and America*. When we first assembled our anthology, John Ashbery was one of our poets. We had miscalculated the length and had to cut pages, and stupidly cut Ashbery. If he had remained, he would not have been a rebel; he would have been an academic poet. Robert Bly and W. S. Merwin, who never taught, appeared in our collection and therefore counted as academics. As a term of abuse, "academic poetry" appears to denigrate schoolteachers and book learning, but the phrase has another source. If a painter was called academic in the nineteenth century, it did not mean that he taught at an art school. The reference was to the Royal Academy and therefore to a tradition—portraits, landscapes, and horses, rendered in many browns—that excluded innovation. In that sense we were indeed academics, whatever we did for a living. Many of us taught at colleges, but eventually so did the Donald Allen poets—Levertov, Ginsberg, Ashbery, Creeley, Duncan, Snyder. The difference was that their poems sought innovation, exploring free verse and eschewing meter. My ideas of poetry came from the poets I loved most: Yeats and Auden, Hardy and Frost, Marvell and Donne, Tate and Ransom, Lowell and Wilbur.

Many of my generation loved the old poets. Early James Wright, Adrienne Rich, Louis Simpson, W. S. Merwin, and Philip Levine were formal and traditional. In order to keep moving, we had to seek different directions. Sometimes a departure came from alien traditions, as when Robert Bly (more than anyone else) discovered and promoted the fantastic, almost surreal images of Spanish-language poets. Galway Kinnell exchanged masters, from Yeats to Whitman. Most of us dropped meter and explored the shapes of free verse, going over to the enemy in the exuberance of the new.

These changes overcame our poetry as we moved into our late twenties and early thirties, and varying trajectories account for our conflicted energies. From *Exiles* I moved into a starker and less decorative line. Later, for many years, I wrote in short-lined enjambed free verse, which specialized in long monosyllables, to conjure dream-images, often ending a poem with an epiphany out of fantasy. I exhausted this vein for myself in the 1960s. For two or three years I felt frustrated, and flailed about seeking a new speech. In the autumn of 1974 I began "Kicking the Leaves" in a long line—my sound entirely altered—that derived from Whitman and poets who followed Whitman—D. H. Lawrence, Theodore Roethke, Galway Kinnell. For decades the dream had excluded the world; now the world came back to my poems. Every time my poetry has changed, the change has begun with a new noise.

Meantime, for thirteen years I was an English teacher. In my eighty years, I have spent only a few as a teacher, and for many decades I have made my living by freelance writing, yet teaching from my late twenties to well into my forties is large in memory. I looked for this kind of work because it seemed a convenient way for a writer to make a living. When my Harvard fellowship was concluding, I looked for a job; the books I had published served instead of a Ph.D. Some Ivy League schools offered instructorships, but they were too close to home. Among literary easterners, it could seem more thrilling to write an essay for *Partisan Review* than to publish a poem in *Poetry*. I wanted to leave that literary culture, and I wanted to get out of New England. In 1957 I left Massachusetts to teach at the University of Michigan. I was twenty-eight, taking a real job for the first time. Shortly I discovered that I loved the classroom and that I flourished there.

In July and August summer school I taught a small introductory literature course that concentrated on American writers. One Monday morning a senior professor led me to my first classroom. I peered into the room through a small pane of glass—so many faces, so many strangers! My guide walked off, gesturing me on. *Don't leave me here! What am I supposed to do?* I had never taught before, and that summer, I spent several hours every day preparing for the next, reading the assignment and sketching out a hundred questions. On the morning before class, I rose at six and worked until nine, cutting my questions down to thirty or forty. When I had asked five or six of them, and answered others, fifty minutes had elapsed and class was over. Answering questions was the best part. Everyone who loves teaching has the same experience: Someone asks a question; it's something you never thought of, but the moment you hear the question you know the answer. Ninety percent of what you say is something you didn't know until you said it. If you are teaching the best literature—I could choose the books I taught—you spend your working hours increasingly intimate with the art you love. You learn by teaching. Those early years, when I felt that I knew a particular book, I would stop teaching it in order to learn about another work that was still mysterious. I taught the American literature class many times, talking my way through the novels of James, Hemingway, Faulkner, and Cather, the poems of Frost, Dickinson, Robinson, and Whitman. In another, sophomore class I offered an introduction to poetry. When the department later cut back on discussion classes, I continued to introduce poetry by lecturing to a hundred non–English majors, poetry's evangelist preaching to convert the diffident. In a more advanced class I lectured to English majors and beginning M.A.s on Yeats and Joyce. However often I taught *Ulysses,* it was always a new book. Whatever I taught, I prepared not by note-taking and preparing questions—once I got over my terror—but by reading the text again, closely, making check marks in the margins. I taught best when I did not prepare a lecture but trusted the flow of the moment. I read aloud to the students with excitement, and improvised explanations for my pleasure. I counted on my passion for the work, stimulated by the presence of the listening faces in front of me. Then I answered questions. If once in two years the enthusiasm did not flow, I would cancel class. My gift to students was not information but demonstration of engagement. Many non–English majors became English majors, doubtless depressing their lifetime incomes.

When I took the Michigan job, I made it a condition that I teach no creative writing. Every term the department gave me a section of freshman composition. It is the hardest class to teach. Twenty students are twenty different sets of difficulty and the difficulty is only partly with writing. My freshmen were away from home for the first time—few came from boarding schools—and struggled with loneliness and liberty. In their essays they expressed or evaded their confusions. Language explains us to ourselves and conceals us from ourselves. Teaching prose style became exploration of the psyche, and I went home from conferences and office hours vibrating with the discomfort and distress of my composition students. (There were contrary elations. When a boy from a northern town suddenly brightens up and understands, or a girl from a high school in suburban Detroit takes fire, the hard class becomes satisfying.) Eventually, debilitated by teaching composition, I volunteered to teach creative writing. To my surprise I liked it—one class a year, ten or twelve people. I could choose the students after checking out their work, and take only those with some facility.

In introductory literary classes, I gave hard books to nineteen-year-olds. One term I assigned Faulkner's *Absalom, Absalom!* and James's *The Ambassadors* and Stevens's *Selected Poems.* I remember students from the first years, lively and irreverent young. Some I still know—grandparents now, sometimes retired. One is a literary critic, praised as an interpreter of Samuel Beckett. Another was a business student and expected to go into his father's firm in Detroit, but dared to undertake literature, which dazzled him. He became devoted to film, worked at the Museum of Modern Art, went to Hollywood, and became CEO of New Line Cinema. Over the millennial midwinter, he hired a French cruise ship to sail down the Amazon to the West Indies, inviting movie producers and writers and directors, friends from his high school, and one old teacher. In my seventies, I drank champagne with Bob Shaye, my student from 1958, gray around the ears, extraordinarily prosperous, still bright and funny.

Shortly after I moved to Ann Arbor, Robert Graves arrived to read his poems. We had coffee at the Michigan Union. I addressed him as "Mr. Graves" and was quickly corrected. "Robert is the name." He knew of me from my time at Oxford. I admired the poet who lived in Majorca and wrote novels to make his living—as well as books about myth and funny ephemera for *Punch.* I felt ashamed to be a teacher rather than a writer, and told him that I envied him writing prose to support himself. Graves asked, "Have you ever tried?" It was a good question. Then I asked him how he had the energy to turn out three or four books a year. Graves had an answer. "The twenty-minute nap," he said. I went home from my coffee with Robert Graves and lay down with a kitchen timer set for twenty minutes. When it clanged I got up, whether I had drowsed or not, and within a week had learned to take a daily short nap, sometimes just drooping down toward dream, to wake with a rush of energy and get to work. I have practiced the twenty-minute nap for half a century. After coffee with Robert Graves, I napped and shortly tried writing *String Too Short to Be Saved,* my first prose book, a recollection of childhood summers on the farm. At first, my prose sounded less like reminiscence than like a book review or a lecture. Over the next year, with difficulty, I hacked out three chapters that began to work.

But I didn't have time enough to throw myself into it. Every morning I worked on poems from six to eight, making a little island of poetry before the oceanic teaching day began. At six, while I drank black coffee and looked at line breaks, I allowed no image of a troubled student to enter my mind. When the clock struck eight, I began my academic duties. Only Andrew interrupted my writing. Every morning a four-year-old came downstairs to play with his father, his red hair nicely topping his blue Dr. Dentons. I discovered a way to please him and get back to my desk. I asked Andrew to commission a poem, to give me a subject. "Toast," he might say. I would make him a couplet, "What the Toast Said":

> It feels so good to be
> Extremely buttery.

I had only to draw something to resemble a slice of toast and he would carry the sheet upstairs to his crib, smiling sweetly, though perhaps still hungry.

Weekends and holidays and summer vacations, I worked first on poems, then on prose: New Hampshire memoir, book reviews, brief literary essays for page two of the *New York Times Book Review*. When Philippa was born five years after Andrew, I tried writing a picture book for her, and wrote it many times, but could never get it right. A publisher bought it anyway, never to publish it—maybe thinking that I would eventually write a real children's book. Andrew gave me a notion that I snapped up. He told me that he had a good, scary idea: He would go to the lion store, buy a lion seed, and grow a lion in a flowerpot on the window seat. In *Andrew the Lion Farmer* the lion is an imaginary friend who plays with Andrew each morning before his parents wake. When the lion goes to seed in the autumn, Andrew collects seeds—to plant next spring his new crop of lions.

Both of my redheaded children engaged my day. The baby seemed preternaturally happy. I carried her to bed every night, and as she grew older she invited me to tickle her. When she was still little, she watched me looking at football on television before I piggybacked her to bed one night. When I set her down, she asked me for "unnecessary roughness"—which became the name of our frolic. Andrew and I sat in the end zone for Michigan football games, and I was studious to explain what was happening on every play. After a disquisition on the single-wing, I asked him, "Do you mind me telling you all this?" "Oh, no," he said, "I don't mind." After a pause, and with perfect benignity, he added, "I'd rather you didn't, but I don't mind."

The small advance for the children's book added to the writing money that I gathered in a savings account. I had the notion that I might buy time off from teaching in order to write. A new source began to provide income. Before coming to Ann Arbor I had done few poetry readings: the Poetry Society of Virginia, the University of Iowa, an arts center in Chicago. Late in the 1950s, poetry readings started to flourish. Until this moment, they had been rare; only Robert Frost did many. Famous poets like Wallace Stevens, Marianne Moore, and William Carlos Williams did one or two a year. Did the poetry reading seem too much an entertainment or performance? The literary scene was stuffy. When William Butler Yeats had crisscrossed America in 1935, a decade after his Nobel, he was not asked to read his poems. He delivered a lecture called "Three Great Irishmen." Maybe it was Dylan Thomas's famous voice that started things. One day my phone rang, a lecture agent asking if he could represent me, selling me to colleges and taking a thirty percent cut. I was amazed. If I sold all of a book's poems to magazines, the pay would not equal the take from one reading. I took to the air, flying out of Detroit on days when I was not teaching, flying Constellations to cities and DC-3s to small towns and smaller colleges.

As a teacher, I read poems aloud in order to win students over to poetry. I wanted to plant a voice in my students' heads by which they could hear poems—Wyatt, Yeats, Frost, Bishop, Marvell—and now I was paid to perform my own work to strangers, strutting on the platform as in my old ambition to be an actor. For years, critics had talked about "a poet's audience," making a metaphor; now the audience was literal, rows and rows of young faces. They were young because the readings were mostly at colleges, but later there were urban poetry festivals, summer conferences, readings in nursing homes and prisons and bars. The skies turned thick with poets traveling to say their lines. As poetry moved to the platform in the United States, the number of literary magazines increased, and the annual number of poetry books, and the sales of individual volumes. With the explosion of M.F.A.s in writing, poetry became more widespread than it had ever been. Its audience did not equal the audience for professional wrestling, but the vogue of the reading multiplied poetry's numbers.

As I read my poems aloud, I paid still more attention to sound in my writing. One morning as I revised, I set down a word that I knew was not right, and I heard myself think: But I can *say* it so that it's right. Immediately, I knew that I had understood one of the hazards of reading aloud. Performance can paper over bad writing, or substitute for the best language. Performance is a problem, and most performance poets or slammers are actors or standup comedians and not poets; we never hear a line break and seldom a new metaphor. There are other problems with the popularity of the poetry reading, but largely the reading has been good for poetry because poets watch their own poems come back to them on the faces of listeners. One addresses not only the Muse but actual people.

Every day I wrote—but I longed to write all day. Having enjoyed six years of fellowships, I decided I should have another fellowship. My second book of poems appeared, *The Dark Houses*, and after two years of teaching I applied for a Guggenheim. When the Guggenheim Foundation turned me down, I was frustrated. My Michigan contract allowed me to take leave without pay. With a wife and two small children, with two thousand dollars in the bank, I took off the forthcoming academic year. I wanted to go back to England and see Oxford friends, but it was too soon to return to Oxford, and London would be too expensive. The English poet Kathleen Raine came to Ann Arbor for a reading. (I had known her in England.) In Michigan, I took the great Luddite on a tour of River Rouge, the Ford factory with its clanging fetor, playing Virgil to her Dante in the hell of modernity. I never saw her face so radiant as it was in those dark Satanic mills. I told her my plans, and speculated about where my family might live. She said that she knew the most beautiful house in England, in England's most beautiful village. Her friend Margaret Bottrall, ex-wife of the poet Ronald, owned a fifteenth-century house called the Priory in the Essex village of Thaxted, which she rented furnished to American airmen stationed at a nearby air base. Her current tenant was leaving, and I rented the Priory for a year.

When the decision was made, and leave granted, I set out to raise more money for the trip. I wrote everyone I knew. Richard Wilbur was general editor for a series of paperbacks devoted to individual poets. He gave me John Greenleaf Whittier to select and introduce for a flat fee. I wrote George Plimpton, who had just been hired by *Horizon* to oversee a group of interviews—dialogue style, like the *Paris Review*'s. He found me three interrogations to do. One subject would be John Gielgud, who declined the favor, but that summer I interviewed Archibald MacLeish, who had been George's teacher and mine, about a play he had just produced. When I was settled in Thaxted I made contact with Henry Moore, who lived only fifteen miles away. We met, I interviewed him for *Horizon*, we played ping-pong, and three years later I sailed back to do his *New Yorker* profile. Without consciousness that I was doing so, I was practicing the life of freelancing.

During the Thaxted year I saw English friends. Geoffrey Hill visited. The freelance life in England was abundant because of BBC Radio. An old Oxford friend, the poet George MacBeth, was a talks producer and signed me up to do Third Programme work. Another producer put me on a weekly Home Service show called *The Critics*. The *New Statesman* hired me to be its poetry critic, and I did essays and reviews for *Encounter*. Its editor was Stephen Spender, who had taken on a *Concise Encyclopedia of Poets and Poetry*—and brought me along as his coeditor at half the fee. Despite this miscellaneous fundraising work, I was able to spend most of my mornings on my poems. After lunch I climbed up to a music room at the back of the Priory which overlooked its vegetable garden—vegetables twelve months a year—and boasted a radiator that I kept warm by feeding coke to a boiler downstairs. I sat on a sofa in the music room every afternoon and finished *String Too Short to Be Saved*. Late in the winter, I rented a Morris Minor station wagon and drove to Rome, where I interviewed Ezra Pound for the *Paris Review*.

In Thaxted my daughter was a baby at the breast, and my son went to public preschool. It was a medieval town of houses mostly attached to each other, pargeting on the stucco fronts, thatch above. When we arrived with trunks from Southampton—those were still the days when we crossed oceans in passenger ships— my family went immediately to bed with head colds. I stepped outside and entered the pub with which we shared a wall. Near the entry a man saluted me with his pint glass and said, "What'll it be?" I thought he had mistaken me for someone he knew, but he hadn't. The village was a friendly place, two thousand souls with half a dozen pubs. We had no car, and walked from baker to greengrocer to butcher. Shortly, we knew almost everybody in town—postmaster and postman, schoolteacher, an Austrian watchmaker, publicans, one of the six businessmen who commuted to London, council house people, vicar, Tory and communist. Chief communist was the priest of the great church on the hill, Father Jack Putterill, a marvelous and shabby diminutive man, full of energy and fun and charity. The Tories in town had motorcars and emigrated to another, more conservative parish on Sundays. They would cross the road to avoid meeting Father Jack on the sidewalk. At first he was cool to us. The Americans who lived in Thaxted were normally stationed at a huge Air Force base called Brize Norton, and their presence in the air above us kept the Cold War close. We met the schoolmaster, George Scrivener, tall and genial grade-school head who had escaped from the poverty of his laboring family by passing tests and getting scholarships. George loved Father Jack and had room in his heart for an American poet and family, and he brought us together with the vicar. Father Jack was son-in-law to the original "Red Vicar," Conrad Noel, who had hoisted the red flag over the church even before the Russian Revolution. Back in the thirties, when Stalin was murdering kulaks and executing old Bolsheviks, someone had the idea of sending Jack to the Soviet Union so that he could see it for himself and clear his head. He came back full of enthusiasm for Russian cathedrals turned antireligious museums.

Early in the century Thaxted had been the site of a medieval revival. William Morris visited, and Cecil Sharp brought Morris dancing here. On every holiday the Thaxted Morris Men danced in front of the church, their performances interrupted by country dancing, like our square dances but without a caller, so that women could take part. Weavers came to Thaxted to weave. There was talk of guilds, and Gustav Holst inhabited a townhouse across from the great fifteenth-century Guildhall. His daughter Imogen lived on, and coached the church's choir. This Thaxted medievalism was a reason Kathleen Raine found it the most beautiful village in England: It was determined to remain old style, and not to join in modernity.

The Guildhall, underneath the church at the top of the hill, headed the main street, which widened beneath it to become the marketplace on Saturdays. Our Priory was opposite the Guildhall, across the wide road from the Holst house. It was astonishing to open the front door in the morning—milk was delivered; the first post of the day was early—and see buildings that looked as they had looked five hundred years earlier. The Priory was three stories high. The ground floor had two small front rooms with fireplaces. (Often I built a coal fire and worked in one of them.) Stairs curved up from the Jacobean newel post, and in back on the ground floor was the kitchen, with a coke stove that I kept burning all the time. Back of the kitchen, on the way to the garden, there was a large room featuring a furnace that burned coal. Mrs. Bottrall had told me that the Priory was centrally heated. But the boiler, as the furnace was called, provided no heat to the ground floor. Upstairs was a bedroom for Andrew, and a bigger bedroom for the rest of the family, looking out at the Guildhall and marketplace. These rooms received slight warmth from one radiator each. Farther into the house on the second floor was an enormous two-story hall, or dining room, with black-and-white Jacobean wall paintings down the interior wall, which we shared with the pub. This room had a fireplace and a single radiator, but under no circumstances was it ever warm. We put the Christmas tree there, and it never dropped a needle. Only once in the spring did we eat there with guests, shivering with two couples, old Oxford friends, on a June day. Past the tall hall, a low doorway, a little over five feet high, led to the music room with its grand piano under a low ceiling with two radiators. It was warm enough to sit there while I wrote prose in the afternoon.

This year, with all its writing, was the best of my life before Jane and New Hampshire. I lived off the land, testing out my unavowed agenda to become a freelance writer. When I sailed home, I still had two thousand dollars in the savings account.

❖

IT WAS A LETDOWN returning to classrooms and faculty meetings, to office hours and papers and cocktails after the game. From six to eight in the morning it was still poetry, and I finished my third book of poems. Sometimes it was hard to get started. To warm up, I began a comic blank-verse narrative—a few lines before going back to free verse—out of a medieval fabliau. I found the old manuscript twenty years later, in New Hampshire, and tried to revise it. Where I sit today, working at my desk, there are shelves behind me that are dense with abandoned or unfinished work—including the book-length mock epic in iambic pentameter. Behind my neck roosts a rookery of bad manuscript. To write as much as I have done, I have needed often to fail. There is another book-length poem behind my neck, ten-line stanzas that look like surrealism but are actually bad dada. Rooting around, I recently found another long collection, written in the sixties in a time of fret and distress. It is what Robert Bly has called light-verse surrealism, and nothing fit to print.

Teaching rather than writing was a letdown, but I returned to Ann Arbor friends. There were professors of English to argue literature with. The novelist Allan Seager, who had been a Rhodes Scholar at Oxford in the 1930s, loved to talk about writing. He had known Theodore Roethke when they taught together at Bennington College, and Allan told good stories. Other friends visited from afar. Robert and Carol Bly lived the low-overhead life on a Minnesota farm without running water, but every winter drove to Manhattan to sublet a flat for a month from a New Yorker who went south. They stopped in Ann Arbor on their way down and on their way back. Poet friends visited and did poetry readings: Galway Kinnell, James Wright, Adrienne Rich, Philip Levine, Gary Snyder. Our houseguests shared a profession. When Andrew was eight or nine, he asked how old he had to be before he could go to poetry school.

There were also town friends—doctors, lawyers, automobile executives—who commuted to Detroit, who had chosen Ann Arbor to live in, rather than Grosse Pointe or Bloomfield Hills, because of the university with its music and theater. There were long conversations in living rooms, a fresh drink always to hand. In these years, I lived the suburban life—wearing neckties to cocktail and dinner parties, swimming and playing tennis at the Racquet Club. The contrast with the quiet of New Hampshire is so extreme that Ann Arbor feels like a remembered dream.

With my young family, in 1959–60, I spent another year in Thaxted—this time with a Guggenheim—where I wrote the *New Yorker* profile of Henry Moore and drafted a play about Robert Frost. *An Evening's Frost* played off-Broadway in 1966. Behind my desk there is a copy of this play. There are also attempts at more prose pieces for *The New Yorker*, never completed. There are bad short stories, children's books, and maybe hundreds of poems that never worked out. Every now and then I do an inventory. Every now and then something that appeared to be dead comes gradually to life. Often it dies again. For the second Thaxted year, the Priory was unavailable. We rented a different house, at the bottom of the market, downhill from the Priory. This time we had a car, and I spent much of the year with Henry Moore, working toward my profile. With the car, I could visit his friends for interviews, and more easily get to the train station for London, where I picked up more BBC work. Wednesday was usually a London day, when John Wain—novelist, poet, literary journalist—came up from Reading to the Salisbury, a magnificent gin palace of a pub, and literary sorts gathered for a pub lunch: Ted Hughes, A. Alvarez.

But bad times took over. After we returned to Ann Arbor, my first marriage ended. For five years I was single, and saw my children only on appointed days. My daily life was troubled, unsettled, full of rash undertaking. I continued to write, but I did not write well. Teaching was the constant, its regularity helping to provide structure to my days, and I spent time with the young—picnics and parties and volleyball. I had always enjoyed the social mix of Michigan students. When I first taught, there were girls named Bobbie Sue with Appalachian accents, daughters of the diaspora that brought workers north to defense plants during the war; there were also boys who belonged to the fraternities that their grandfathers belonged to—old Michigan families for whom Ann Arbor was the Athens where they studied when they were young. The breath of the coming counterculture was at first faint to perceive. Some girls wore long straight hair, no makeup, and black leotards; they were bohemian, some-times known as beatniks. I smelled my first whiffs of marijuana. Ten years later it was Vietnam and acid, rock music and protest. Fucking in the streets demonstrated political protest. When I introduced poetry in 1958, I could reach everyone with Richard Wilbur. By 1968, if I needed to wake up a class, I used D. H. Law-rence. Students reading "Look! We Have Come Through" were reminded of recent drug experiences.

Ann Arbor was lively and the times were rebellious. Robert Bly and David Ray started Poets Against the War, and I stood on many platforms — with Bly and John Logan, with Ed Sanders and Ted Berrigan — to take part in the antiwar movement. I was no leader, yet somebody must have thought I was. I was audited by the IRS six years out of seven. A naval intelligence officer came calling because I refused to write a reference for an old student. As we chatted, the man in uniform opened a file and read aloud a list of petitions I had signed and meetings I had attended. Naïve in my politics, I thought he was being indiscreet. Daniel Ellsberg let me know that I was being harassed. Tom Hayden and Carl Oglesby were my students. Carl brought me to a meeting of SDS leaders and I sat mute, bored witless as five or six young men argued Marxist theology. After an hour or two, Carl took pity and led me aside. "Come on, Don. Let's talk about *poetry*." One day a young woman from back east telephoned that she needed to stay with me for a few days. She was on the lam, she told me, having poured blood over the files of a draft board. She hitchhiked to my house and after three or four days hitchhiked onward. When I returned from leaving her at the highway, I found a middle-aged man knocking at my front door. He wore a brown fedora, a white shirt, a striped tie, a brown suit, and brown shoes. He showed me his badge, FBI, and asked me about Trim Bissell. (No one ever contacted me about the hitchhiker, who enjoyed being on the lam.) Trim was an old student of mine who blew up a draft board in Seattle—at night; no one was hurt. He had visited Ann Arbor while he was out on bail and I had written him a check, permitting the FBI to seek me out after he jumped bail. The agent asked me if I had seen Trim lately, or knew where he was. I didn't. We talked a little. Then the FBI man stood up and took a piece of paper from his coat pocket. Standing, he read me aloud the Harboring Act before he drove away.

Dan Ellsberg came to Ann Arbor once a year and stayed at my house as he defended the government at teach-ins. Then Dan turned antiwar with serious results. He sat in my living room one afternoon telling me about a top-secret study of the Vietnam War that he had photocopied at the Rand Corporation. It was explosive stuff, he said, but he did not know what he could do with it. He had approached a senator who would not touch it. Maybe he could release it to a newspaper? Maybe the *New York Times* . . . ? I was bored. Dan had a way, when he was possessed by a subject, of going on and on. As soon as he paused long enough, I changed the subject to something more interesting, like poetry. Months later the newspapers erupted with a story about the release of secret papers on Vietnam. At first, the name of the photocopier was not public knowledge. It took me two days to realize that it was Dan—doing, with courage, what he had told me about.

❖

WITH THE EXPENSES of a divorce, I looked for freelance work to help with money. One day I was astonished to hear from my literary agent that Little, Brown wanted me to write a handbook for freshman English. (Later I discovered that he had equally astonished Little, Brown by telling them that I wanted to write such a handbook.) Because I had taken up teaching creative writing, I no longer taught composition, but I remembered it well, and I had strong ideas about prose style. I began the textbook called *Writing Well,* not a handbook but a guide to diction, sentences, and paragraphs. The best section is called "Words." Later in the book, to make it saleable in the market for such texts, I had to work up chapters on rhetorical forms like Argumentation, Definition, and Comparison and Contrast. I hated writing these chapters, but *Writing Well*—which first appeared in 1973 and went through nine editions—sold well and allowed me to quit the university and move with Jane Kenyon to the farm in New Hampshire. We had met when she was my student in 1969, and married three years later.

❖

WRITING WELL was a success, but there were large failures—I have mentioned some—among my attempts at writing. One such failure leaves a story for telling. Early in the 1970s, I spent two years working on a biography of the actor Charles Laughton, who had died in 1962. I spent months talking with his widow in Hollywood, interviewed dozens of film people, received a Guggenheim for support, made two trips to England for interviews, accumulated half a million words of draft—and abandoned the book when Laughton's widow responded with loathing to a sample I showed her.

Charles Laughton won the Academy Award in 1933 for *The Private Life of Henry VIII*. His wife and widow was the English actress and singer Elsa Lanchester, best known as the heroine of *The Bride of Frankenstein;* she survived her husband by two decades. Laughton became internationally celebrated as a movie star when Alexander Korda cast him as Henry VIII. Laughton specialized in grotesques. He played the hideous and tender Quasimodo in *The Hunchback of Notre Dame* and the sadistic Captain Bligh in the original *Mutiny on the Bounty*. But actors' names are writ in water, and if I speak Laughton's name today, people who are not cineastes or theater professionals have difficulty placing it. In 1973, in the dead man's living room, I asked his widow if she still had the Oscar statuette from forty years before. She brought the trophy from the cellar, covered with dust. It had done duty as a doorstop, she said, but then its surface began to peel away.

❖

IT WAS IN 1970 or 1971 that I had a telephone call from a literary agent in New York, telling me that I wanted to write a biography of Charles Laughton.

"What?"

I had seen Laughton's movies when I was young and remembered him well, but I had never followed film, movie stars, or Hollywood. My agent told me that Elsa Lanchester had approached her agency wanting someone to write an honest biography, not a Hollywood hack job. She wanted her husband's homosexuality brought into the open, because it was central to his character and career. My agent had suggested likely writers, one after another, and when Lanchester read their work she turned them all down. Frustrated, my agent remembered that Lanchester loved country books, and showed her *String Too Short to Be Saved*—and when she read it, Elsa decided that I should write the biography.

I was skeptical if not incredulous, but my agent asked me to think it over. I remained doubtful, but I needed money. The publisher with whom Lanchester had already signed a contract—as the source of information, she would collaborate with any biographer—flew me to Hollywood to talk with her. Elsa Lanchester charmed me, and cooked for lunch a clever omelet. When she summarized her husband's life, I was won over.

Born in 1899 in Scarborough, North Yorkshire, Laughton developed early a talent for acting but did only local amateur theater because his family was adamant that he take over the business they had built up. At the late age of twenty-five, he escaped to the Royal Academy of Dramatic Art in London, and in two years was acclaimed as a stage actor in the West End. After his movie success as Henry VIII, Charles came to Hollywood and his greatest fame—not only *Hunchback* and *Mutiny*, but *Ruggles of Red Gap* and other successes—but a decade later his career was in collapse. *Captain Kidd* exploited his Captain Bligh, and later his career dwindled into the degradation of *Abbott and Costello Meet Captain Kidd.* Lanchester told me he took on miserable roles because he needed money to pay young lovers and their blackmail. Late in life his movie career perked up with two good movies, and he made popular tours giving public readings of literature, but his descent was clear. As I listened to Lanchester tell Laughton's story, I made a gesture with my right hand, the inverted U of the tragic semicircle. Elsa blanched. "That's just what Charles did," she said.

Over the next two years I watched all of Laughton's movies, the powerful imprints of his great roles and the fatuous sequels. Some great scenes came from a film that didn't get made. Three years after Laughton's death, BBC Television produced a documentary called *The Epic That Never Was*, about a film of *I, Claudius* that Alexander Korda tried to produce in 1937. Laughton played the title role of an obscure Roman emperor. Korda imported as director Josef von Sternberg, the director of Marlene Dietrich in *The Blue Angel* and a notorious disciplinarian who wore riding boots on the set. As filming went on, Laughton did brilliant scenes only to blow take after take. *The Epic That Never Was* showed rushes, saved from abandoned film, of Laughton playing the bumbling emperor who limped and stammered, constantly humiliated. In close-ups Laughton's lips flap as he stammers, his great eyes roll and his cheeks shudder; then he would forget lines and spoil the take. Because of Laughton's mistakes, cost overruns became mountainous, and Korda bulldozed the mountain. Elsa Lanchester believed Laughton flubbed because of Sternberg's cruelty on the set. Sternberg made continual cutting allusions to Laughton's homosexuality.

On the publisher's advance, I went to Los Angeles during time away from teaching, and took a year's leave without pay. Lanchester was helpful, but she was hard to work with. She put down almost everyone she spoke of. She would speak movingly of Charles the actor and thinker, whom she admired with passion, and then deride Charles the man, her contempt as vivid as her admiration. Her emotions were complex, and her life had been improbable. Elsa had little schooling. She danced, and found herself in her teens as a student of Isadora Duncan in Paris. (Duncan was a charlatan, Elsa said.) When the young Elsa returned to London, she entertained in nightclubs, singing as well as dancing. "I never wanted to be an *actress*," she told me. "I wanted to be *notorious*." She graduated from nightclubs to the stage, playing in reviews and in dramas. When Laughton began to act in the West End, Lanchester was better known than he. They watched each other perform before they met; then they were cast together in a play. Elsa was drawn to Charles the actor. Charles was drawn to Elsa's eccentricity and contempt for convention. They became lovers, as Charles successfully denied the direction of his sexuality, and lived together. Then, a couple of years after they were married, blackmail forced Charles to confess to Elsa that he had afforded himself an Indian waiter on their living room sofa. Laughton eventually devoted himself entirely to men, and so did Lanchester. In the 1940s there were rumors, and studios urged the couple to have a child. With Elsa, Charles could not produce an erection, and Elsa told him with scorn—she mimicked herself, telling me—"You're *homosexual!*"

For two years I flew in and out of Hollywood, reading and writing and interviewing. I pored over papers and took notes as I talked with her. I was there to work, and there were no further omelets. She had a second house, overlooking the sea at Santa Monica, which Charles had bought because it was next to Christopher Isherwood's house, where he lived with his partner Don Bachardy. "I want to be among my own kind," said Charles. Elsa told this story as an example of Charles's late acceptance of his sexuality. Today, long after Stonewall, Charles's secrecy or guilt may seem cowardly. But his origins were Victorian, north of England, Catholic. Born to a family of modest means, he strove to acquire respectability—and if he had come out of the closet, there would have been no films at all.

In 1972 and 1973 I traveled to England to do interviews for the biography. I talked to a barrister-playwright who revealed that it was he who bought off a judge when Charles was blackmailed by the Indian waiter. I interviewed an old classmate from Charles's Jesuit boarding school, Stonyhurst, which the adult Charles remembered with loathing. Just before the 1973 trip, at Elsa's entreaty I showed her some of what I had written. I roughed out an initial hundred pages from the manuscript of half a million words. It was a stupid thing to do, and I did it stupidly. If I had waited a year, my hundred pages would have turned into an appropriate twenty. As it was, my prose overacted: I had been moved by Elsa's repeated accounts of Charles's death from cancer. I told details about diagnosis in Michigan, a miserable flight across country on a stretcher straddling rows of first-class seats. When Elsa told me a story, she spoke with all her dramatic skill. When my paragraphs repeated what she had told me, Elsa found the passage melodramatic, forced, morbid . . .

At a London hotel I received a telegram from my agent in New York, telling me Lanchester was enraged: *The book would never do.* I flew home early and telephoned her: I would fly out to Hollywood; we would talk about our differences. In a cold voice Lanchester told me not to come; I would not enter her house. Eventually her long letter arrived, addressed to the publisher, and an annotated copy of the hundred pages. She said I had made her husband out to be a silly old poof and herself a monster. She made errors reading; I quoted a long passage directly from her voice on tape, using quotation marks, as she described a theatrical production. Forgetting or ignoring that I quoted her, Elsa wrote in the margin, "This shows that Donald knows nothing about theater." Eventually, I think I would have written a good book, massive with extremes of triumph and guilt, contempt and adoration. But I would not be permitted to write it. Although I had worked hard, I accepted my failure with relative ease, which may suggest that I was glad to be out of it. I sighed for a day or two, put the manuscript away, and began a reminiscence of the great poets I had known in my youth. For two years, I had written the biography that never was.

❖

MEANWHILE, I continued to enjoy evangelizing for literature in the classroom, but I no longer learned so much by teaching. When someone asked me a question, I had already given the answer; I played the tape. I became aware of colleagues around me who were burned out, suffering boredom compounded by tenure. After ten years on the job, it fell to me to begin to chair committees, and I am bad at chairing committees. At the same time, the university as an institution came to annoy me. Decisions at all universities are ultimately financial. The University of Michigan inherited a beautiful federal house in downtown Ann Arbor, which sat on valuable square footage; the house was torn down for a fast-food franchise. Under an enlightened dean, and with a grant from the Ford Foundation, UM had started a clone of Harvard's original, a Michigan Society of Fellows. I was a senior fellow, and watched—protesting and impotent—as a subsequent dean destroyed it because Michigan was a democratic institution and must not be elitist. (Think of an egalitarian Society of Fellows.) Then the English department imploded—terrible fights at department meetings, conservative senior professors shouting "Resign, resign!"—with allegations of illicit acts by committee chairmen. A couple of years later, when Jane urged me to leave my job in order to live in New Hampshire, and write full time, I was ready. I would miss the classroom. I would miss certain students. I would miss friends, but I would not miss the university.

The move, however, was not a departure but an arrival. I traveled to solitude with Jane in the New Hampshire house, to a life of poetry, to the desk and the shelves behind my neck, to twenty-minute naps, to pounding out three or four books a year—traveling from Robert Graves and coffee at the Michigan Union.

Grief's House

IT WAS EARLY IN OUR MARRIAGE, before Jane and I moved to New Hampshire, that my biography of Charles Laughton imploded. Shortly thereafter we left the academic city and lived together at the farmhouse for twenty years. I wrote a book about our marriage, about her illness and death. *The Best Day the Worst Day* began as the middle of this memoir, but when my publishers read the whole manuscript, they realized that the midsection ought to be published by itself. They were right—but this book suffers from a hole in the middle. Because I have spoken out of my experience for most of my writing life, *Unpacking the Boxes* repeats patches of earlier writing. In *Life Work* and *Fathers Playing Catch with Sons*, I have written about my father—a salient character early in these pages. In the poems of *The Old Life*, I told stories repeated here. A book of poems called *Without* tells of Jane's illness and death—and also of grief.

After Jane died, grief's house replaced the house of love and poetry. For fifteen months there had been nothing in the world but leukemia. We had faced death daily for more than a year, and we had said everything to each other that we could think of saying. Now the active presence of her dying was replaced by the vacancy of her absence. That I had been her constant caregiver left me with a sort of comfort. I knew I had done the right things—auditing her pills, infusing her with chemicals through her heart catheter, bringing her warm blankets—but now there was nothing to replace the caregiving. A huge emptiness took over the house. I visited her grave and talked to her. I did what I had to do—shopping, attending my three-year-old granddaughter's birthday party, selling Jane's car—but I cannot reconstruct those early days as if they progressed in human time. At some point I started writing a poem out of her death, trying to use language the way Jane would have done. *What would Jane say? How would Jane have written about my death?* I hung her photographs on the study wall in back of my desk, two decades of pictures from the twenty-four-year-old I married to the beautiful woman late in her forties who would shortly contract leukemia. I could not touch her clothes except to take her winter coats from pegs by the front door and lay them in a guest room upstairs alongside her mother's and my mother's, both of whom had died during Jane's illness. Jane's bathrobe hung behind the bathroom door for more than a year. Her thick nearsighted glasses lay on the table at her side of the bed—months later, I gave her eyeglasses to Alice Mattison, Jane's closest friend, who has eye trouble that Jane fretted over—as well as her watch that we bought together in Rome. I used Jane's watch when I broke my own, which Jane had given me as an anniversary gift. She had engraved the back: "PERKINS 4-17-72 MORE LOVE 4-17-87." (She called me by the pet name of Perkins. Early in our New Hampshire life, we had driven through Perkins Cove in Maine, where the stores and streets were all named Perkins. "This Perkins must have been quite a fellow," said Jane, and began to call me by that name.) My watch broke when, shortly after her death, I dropped it in the parking lot of a restaurant, and when I found it in gravel a day later, a car had crushed it. The first jewelry store I visited told me it was irreparable and I wept before an embarrassed clerk. Another jewelry store found used parts and I wore my PERKINS watch again.

Time was an issue, hours and the calendar: For months I obsessed about the days of the week. Saturday was the day she died; every Tuesday it was the Tuesday when we found out she would die; Wednesday was the day when we buried her. I kept track of how many weeks had gone by since each of these events. Saturdays I regularly burst into tears at 7:57 A.M., the moment of death. (Twice, after I had wiped my eyes, I discovered that I was an hour early, and would have to cry again.) At first I found it difficult to leave the house. I drove to Vermont overnight but woke up in desperation at four in the morning to return. This house contained her, and I paced its rooms up and down. I moved furniture in the living room, undoing arrangements that accommodated her illness—her blue chair next to mine as we watched movies together. Walking up and down, often I howled. No one would hear me, deep in the country, to dial 911. My outbursts frightened our dog Gus, who wondered what he had done wrong. He searched for Jane everywhere and asked me to fetch her back. Several times each day, he brought me one of her shoes—slippers or sneakers—and set it on the floor beside me. At least once a day my mind expected to see her when I turned a corner. From time to time I took a note in a blank book that Jane had given me:

Today she has been dead a month. When our minister Alice Ling prayed with us, grace entered the hospital room, or our bedroom at Eagle Pond, or by telephone in the Seattle apartment. Otherwise, God did not manifest Himself.

Jesus loves me, this I know.
His house is in the village though.

When you most need belief or faith, faith appears most wish-
fulfillment. Deus Absconditus.

I never daydreamed that she heard me. Because I wanted so
much to believe in an afterlife, I did not permit myself to enter-
tain the notion. When people reminded me that she was waiting
for me in paradise, I remained polite and uncomforted. My only
companionship was with death-people, never with optimists or
death-deniers. People came calling, old students and editors
and women friends of ours. One woman belittled grief. "Dead
is dead," she told me, but most of my visitors brought their own
grief with them. Adrienne Rich spent the middle of a day; Sharon
Olds visited with Bobbie Bristol. I told my callers stories about
her illness and dying, an ancient mariner required to repeat, over
and over, "I closed her eyes." In thought and speech and dreams
and letters, I dwelt entirely on the last days—lifting her onto the
potty, the final word she spoke, the way her hands clutched beside her ears. After two months, I reached further back, but not
so far back as health. I inhabited again the many hospital rooms
in New Hampshire, and in Seattle where she underwent a bone
marrow transplant and we rented an apartment near the hospital.
I drove with her again to Emergency. I saw in my mind only the
bald Jane of leukemia. It was more than a year before I could re-
call Jane healthy and energetic, with her dominant hair, with her
ribald tongue and laugh, with her devotion to flowers and poetry.
    When I wept, Gus tried to comfort me. At night when I went to
bed, he slept on Jane's side. He longed for me to go to bed, and

after supper often suggested it, herding me toward the bedroom. While I was flossing my teeth during the sixth inning, or getting into my nightshirt, I would reassure him out loud that we were about to lie down. One night I told him cheerfully, "Okay. Come on, Gus. It's deadtime." I had made slips of the tongue ever since the first days of her illness: "My life has leukemia." Once I was telling a visitor about March 13, 1995, when Jane felt momentarily better and we stopped at a Dairy Queen. Jane tried to eat—I told my friend—a "peanut buster barfait."

There were slips that were not of the tongue. A few months after the funeral I went to Concord to receive an award for my children's books. Earlier, when Jane was living, I had told the International Reading Association that I could not attend, because I would not leave her side. Her death permitted me to accept their invitation. Barry Moser drove from western Massachusetts to speak in my honor. The announcement said that the presentation was scheduled for a Concord restaurant at six-thirty, so I planned to drop in on my daughter Philippa and the two granddaughters on the way. As I turned onto I-93, a New Hampshire state policeman stopped me. The new stickers were missing from my license plates. He was polite when I gave him my license and registration. He found the stick-ons attached to the registration, and affixed them himself. I drove off and in a moment he was flashing at me again and pulling me over to the side of the road. He had not returned my license and registration. After visiting with Philippa and the girls, I left in plenty of time to get to the awards ceremony at six-thirty—and at the restaurant found everyone finishing dinner and alarmed by my absence. They start things early in New Hampshire, and I had neglected to notice that drinks were at four, dinner at five, and Barry's talk at six-thirty. The kitchen assembled a plate for my dinner.

These errors were my comedy. I knew that I was supposed to be angry at her for leaving me. When I backed my new car into her Saab and took out a headlight, closing her eyes again, I laughed at myself: "That will serve her right." Not comic were the nightmares. Repeatedly I dreamed she had left me for another man. Usually in my dream this abandonment happened while we were courting. In one dream I protested: "But we're getting married," and she answered, with a locution impossible to Jane, "You've got another think coming!" Always she left me because she preferred someone else, and because I was unkind or uncaring. Each nightmare remained with me for days, like an afterimage on the retina, and turned into waking groundless jealousies out of our past. When I put the nightmares together with my erotic fantasies, I understood that I expressed anger in sexual terms: "You abandoned me. Here's what you get."

My fantasies about other women began while she was alive. When she was first diagnosed, for as long as a month I was assaulted by daydreams of making love to other women. In a persistent scenario, Jane was dead and I played the field. Never mind that I was old, never mind that I was sick with dread over the woman I loved. The fantasies were adolescent, of naïve abundant sexual adventure, and they interrupted my anxiety with a leering insistence, as if to offer compensation for Jane's possible death. But I was not about to betray her; I came on to nobody, undertook nothing. Maybe these fantasies sought distraction, but they only supplied further pain in their repetitious folly. Then they went away. A year later, when we learned that Jane would die, they returned in all their urgency, to disappear after two days as Jane slipped down toward death. A week or two after she died the same scenarios returned, interrupting not dread but grief, and they were louder and more obsessive than ever. They were not cheerful concupiscence; they ripped at my spirit as much as the nightmares did. But two weeks after she died I bought condoms.

My sleeping brain went everywhere. In predictable anxious dreams, not quite nightmares, I mismanaged her medications, and woke in panic to remember: It's all right; she's dead! In one dream my responsibility was not limited to the death of my wife. Jane had just died in our big house, which in the dream was deep in the woods. Neighbors who lived roundabout were sorry for me in my loss, and even more sorry that I had to go to jail. The sheriff was coming to arrest me because I had devoted all my attention to Jane, so that the old women who lived alone in their cottages, lacking my attentions, had starved to death.

From the blank book:

Three months ago today. Fourteen weeks ago today. I keep busy. I am doing the 1994 Income Tax, painful because eleven of these months are leukemia. I walk the dog, write poems, cull and sort my books in the effort to organize this house still disfigured by unattended and uninvestigated materials that accumulated while she was sick. I answer the thousand letters of commiseration. My solitude is almost perfect. I visit the grave. I look at her pictures and speak to her. I keep so busy, I seldom explore my grief in daydream. In another night dream she came back from the dead and died again. When I write every morning, making poetic lines about pain is a way of avoiding pain. Or maybe I transfer my pain onto others. Or maybe it's what Coleridge said in a notebook: "Poetry—excites us to artificial feelings—makes us callous to real ones." I turned my memories and feelings into language and by old habit tried to make my words into art—into the object called a poem, something that may exist outside my messy self and its pains or angers in the granite of art.

Today there was a photo session, photographs to publicize my first poetry reading in nineteen months. The young man drove up from Hartford and posed me for two hours against daylilies and barnboards. For two hours I neither spoke nor kept busy, which allowed or forced me to go inside and fall victim to what happened there. My ruminations turned wholly morbid. I obsessed on her body in its grave, on the absolute darkness of her box, where no light could enter to reflect the whiteness of the salwar kameez that covered her cold body. What color was her skin today? Then my mind obsessed on ants. In the sandy soil over her grave are dozens of small hills thriving with tiny ants. How well is the coffin sealed? Probably ants don't travel six feet down but I could not stop imagining that tiny ants gained entrance to her coffin and removed her body atom by atom. Especially I thought of them eating her lips. My mind kept repeating a jingle that off-rhymed two monosyllables, hitting them hard like the heel-words in a jump-rope rhyme: "Those are ants / That eat her lips."

Whenever I met someone, I talked about Jane. If I went to a diner for lunch, or sat at a bar, and a stranger said, "Please pass the salt," I passed it and said, "My wife used to salt everything, even ham. She died of leukemia, fifteen months after she got it. She was only forty-seven. She was in good shape, climbed Mount

Washington the summer before, then suddenly . . ." Everybody had to know, and everybody had to know everything. It didn't matter whether the person I talked to seemed interested or not. There were those who remained silent, disapproving or embarrassed, unable to say a word. I kept talking. Sometimes people I knew avoided me because death was something they needed to evade. Once I walked in the supermarket and watched a man turn away, pretending not to see me. I was death's presence. The man who turned away was minister in a big church. Much help he must have been to grieving survivors.

One morning I had a note from a friend in Seattle, a nurse who had tended Jane during her bone marrow transplant. Maggie Fisher was pregnant! As with all grievers, my first thought was how pleased Jane would be to hear the news. So I wrote Jane a letter, telling her about Maggie, and how I had lunch with her friend Joyce, and about our dog Gus. I was happy, writing Jane a letter with line breaks. After the first took shape, I began a second, "Midsummer Letter," then another for the first autumn of her death—and on and on through "Letter after a Year." Then I stopped. I didn't stop writing poems of grief, but I could no longer address her as Jane, and "she" replaced "you." In the frantic year after her death I was happy only once a day—when I sat at my desk in the morning, writing her or writing about her. When I ran out of poetic steam, each morning, and stood up at my desk, I knew I had to get through twenty-two hours before I could be happy again. Every day I redrafted what I had done before. Writing to Jane and about her kept me going: the poetry habit that had been our first and continued connection. The rest of the day, I stayed connected to Jane's own poems as I worked with her publisher on her posthumous *Otherwise*, and collaborated on the tributes people planned for her: New York, Cambridge, Minneapolis, Washington. For twenty years I had been forbidden to promote her work, because she feared that she would seem to profit from my advocacy. She couldn't stop me now.

As I visited her grave every day, almost every day I found messages left there for Jane from people who came to the site in homage. Someone left behind a huge fungus, the kind that grows on sick trees or dead ones. There were poems to Jane, and letters: "I never knew you, Jane, but . . ." There were little gifts: crockery animals, dogs and cats, flowers in pots, and stones shaped like hearts or perfectly round. I noticed these items and felt comforted by the devotion of others, and then I noticed that gradually, one at a time, these little objects disappeared. The grave's visitors not only left something behind but took something away—a souvenir from Jane Kenyon's grave. One time I visited with a poet from Ohio who was staying with me. As she stood in front of Jane's grave, she pulled off one of her earrings and placed it on the top of the stone. I was moved by what she did, but I needed to tell her, "Someone will take it, in memory of Jane." She said she knew it, and it was all right. The earring was gone within a week. When Gus died, I scattered his ashes on Jane's grave as I had told her I would do, and left behind his collar. People don't come so often now, and the collar is still there.

Earlier, I had set out to work toward Jane's graveyard monument. I telephoned stone carvers in Laconia, recommended by our funeral parlor, and a man visited me with sample stones and a book of typefaces. I knew what I wanted: polished black granite inscribed in white. Galway Kinnell and Bobbie Bristol suggested that I engrave lines from Jane's "Afternoon at MacDowell." In 1992 we had gone to the MacDowell Colony when Richard Wilbur received the annual gold medal. I was skinny, doing chemo, waiting for my cancer to return; earlier that year, half my liver had been removed. Jane wrote about sitting under the canopy, listening to musicians and to Wilbur reading his poems, watching the sun go in and out of the clouds, worrying about losing me. She ended the poem:

> After music and poetry we walk to the car.
> I believe in the miracles of art, but what
> prodigy will keep you safe beside me,
> fumbling with the radio while you drive
> to find late innings of a Red Sox game?

The monument man and I made the decisions: size and shape; smooth top and sides, the base left rough. I picked type from his book of samples. Casually he remarked that he'd do the names in serif with the poetic lines in sans serif. I remembered, thank goodness, that Jane had disliked the mixture of serif and sans serif. In a week or two the mockup arrived, actual size, and I made adjustments. I showed it to Philippa and a few visitors, then returned it with my check. Installation was guaranteed for the end of August. I hoped it would be there before snow closed the graveyard for winter.

In the blank book I wrote about our nurses at Hitchcock:

> Tonight our nurse Kate McKay had me to dinner to read aloud
> Jane's poems to five of Jane's nurses and helpers. Kate's house
> is large and beautiful, isolated and stately, Federal and built in
> 1760, a mile and a half uphill from Grafton. Kate keeps horses

there, as well as dogs and cats. Margie Cole was there, the social worker who let me weep on her shoulder a year ago. There was Mary Roach, the most articulate/tender of all the nurses. There were Lynn Daly, Karen Hewett, and Sharon Van Brunt who drove one hour from Hitchcock to Kate's, after finishing their twelve-hour shifts. Three male nurses were on night shifts and couldn't come. Kate made shish kebab and I read them Jane's poems. When I read "The Shirt," Mary exploded in lascivious laughter. Late in the evening, I boasted about the thousand letters I had received. Sharon Van Brunt needed to say that, when she was taking care of Jane, she didn't know she was a poet; Jane was Jane.

Ahead of me lay my first reading. In the years after our move to New Hampshire I had read my poems hundreds of times. Now I was nervous to mount the platform again, and feared that I could not maintain my composure. The *Hartford Courant* was a sponsor of the Hill-Stead Museum's series of summer readings, outdoors in its Sunken Garden, and I agreed to write an essay for its Sunday magazine that would appear before the reading. In the article I wrote about making poems out of personal wretchedness:

My wife Jane Kenyon and I made up a joke that we repeated as occasion arose. It parodied a poet's Christmas letter: "I had a tough year. My book got bad reviews, Phyllis ran off with my editor, and our kids died when the house burned. But I got some poems out of it."

Young poets sometimes fear, as they begin a life in art, that personal history may become mere material, as if one lived one's life in order to write about it. When I was twenty

I broke up with a girlfriend after three years. Driving home in tears, I was appalled when a line for a poem popped into my head. (I wasn't so appalled that I didn't write the poem.) Sometimes, as in the parody, an artist flaunts an exploitative attitude. But as a poet ages, subject to inevitable losses, it becomes appropriate to write out of grief—appropriate, necessary, therapeutic. Over fifteen months of Jane's illness, I loved caring for her, tucking her up in a tender quilt. My principal comfort was to comfort her—but I took comfort as well in continuing to write, even as she lay beside me, poems derived directly from her suffering.

Eventually, the writing is not only for the writer's sake. A poem is nothing if it is not beautiful, a work of art that pleases the senses and resolves manyness into a whole shape. But a poem may be soul-comfort as well as body-comfort. In depression, Jane wrote to comfort herself and as a result she comforted others. People go to Jane's poems for succor. The beauty of art is only a first (albeit ineluctable) requirement. Poems may comfort the afflicted—by their beauty of sound, by humor, by intelligence or wisdom, by the pleasures of resolution, by exact rendering of emotion, and by the embrace of common feeling.

Galway Kinnell was the most tender of my male friends when Jane died. He drove six hours from Vermont to Connecticut to introduce me at the Sunken Garden. I began by reading some poems by Jane. Among my own poems I read an early version of "Weeds and Peonies," the first poem I began after her death. The sponsors told me that three thousand people were there. There were lights in front of me, so that I could see only twenty or thirty faces in the garden's darkness on an immaculate August night. I felt eerie, heavy with grief and addressing a populated darkness. But it felt good to stand up and say her poems and mine.

As the summer dragged itself on, friends looked after me. Galway Kinnell and Bobbie Bristol spent summers and holidays in Vermont, two and a half hours away. Sometimes we met for dinner halfway, in Norwich, Vermont. I gave Bobbie the cashmere sweats that were my last Christmas present to Jane. The two of them drove to my house months later, winter, and we visited the grave together, using their studded tires to drive over ice and snow. Kendel Currier, my assistant, has been central to my endurance of life after Jane. She is my cousin—her great-grandmother was my grandfather's sister—and she began typing my dictated letters the summer when Jane was first sick. She put my manuscript in her computer, and later, when she was looking for a place to live, moved into the cottage seventy yards down the road, which Jane and I had bought fifteen years before. She became my bookkeeper, paying bills and keeping accounts. She also read manuals, showing me how to work my machines, and made telephone calls to solve problems in cable television, travel, and finance. When I was in New York and lost my glasses in my apartment, I called her for advice on where to look. Most important, she was a friend when I was at my lowest, a shoulder to weep on, an advocate and counselor only seventy yards away. That she was a woman, and not a lover, was essential to the comfort she gave me.

Our Seattle nurse, pregnant Maggie Fisher, and her husband came calling at Eagle Pond Farm. I wanted to show them Jane's grave, and regretted that the stone would not be there. When we drove into the graveyard, it had just been installed. As I looked at the new gravestone in its starkness, I understood why I had wanted polished black marble with white letters. In Washington Jane and I had gazed for an hour at the Vietnam Memorial.

JANE KENYON   DONALD HALL

1947–1995   1928–

I BELIEVE IN THE MIRACLES OF ART BUT WHAT

PRODIGY WILL KEEP YOU SAFE BESIDE ME

Until snow blocked the lane into the graveyard, I visited her marker once or twice a day, often with Gus. The sugar maples across the middle of the cemetery began changing late in August and turned brilliant in the astonishment of late September. Every few days there would be new vegetative tribute at the grave: from early pansies and cut flowers through pots of chrysanthemums and cosmos, as well as a McIntosh apple and a pumpkin. I saw no one at the grave but conversed with nameless visitors. Someone figured a cross out of pinecones; I surrounded it with a pinecone heart. Then snow fell and the road was closed; once or twice in the winter I parked on Route 4 and hiked and slid over the snow to her grave, but it was not safe; suppose you slipped and hit your head on a stone. Apparently I wanted to live. Sometimes I didn't. In my misery I daydreamed suicide. I would burn the house down around me, the house that was almost as dear to me as my wife. I would put a candle in a saucer of gasoline, near wood that had dried for two centuries. I took the cat and the dog with me to Jane's room, and the .22 my father gave me. I shot our cat and dog, and waited for flames. If I couldn't stand being burnt, I had the gun with me. But never did I buy gasoline; suicidal ideation was sufficient. I had only to think of my children and grandchildren to change my daydreaming devices.

It's a common observation that, after the death of a spouse, the griever takes on characteristics of the dead one. To fill the vacancy? To bring the dead back? Writing, I tried to use Jane's language. In the autumn after Jane's death I found myself standing by the bird feeder with her Peterson guide in my hand. The birds had been Jane's preserve for twenty years at the farm. I thought birds were just fine, I loved their song, but I didn't know one from another. As November deepened into December, I found myself suffering from the darkness. Jane's mood always sunk low when the day diminished into December's blackness. Playing the part of her opposite, I used to argue with her that the dark was cozy. In the year of her death, Jane's seasonal affective disorder visited me, and I moved her light box from her study to the top of my desk.

Then, thirteen months after her death, I went manic. I took over Jane's bipolarity along with her diction and her birdsong. I slept only a few hours a night and felt charged all day with energy. After a New Hampshire reading I finished signing books at ten-thirty. I had to be in Connecticut the next day, so I drove directly to New Haven, arriving at three in the morning, waking full of ginger four hours later. At home I packed Jane's clothes and UPS'd them to Rosie's Place in Boston, a refuge for homeless women that Jane had supported. I wept as I stuffed her dresses and jeans, blouses and shirts and saris into garbage bags, but I worked rapidly, ten or twelve hours in a row. Continually high, eating little, I lost twenty pounds. After a Jane memorial in New York, nineteen of us ate at a restaurant together, and I insisted on paying for everybody's dinner. Indeed I was grateful to everybody, but my extravagance was manic.

Another extravagance was erotic. Acting out my fantasies, I pursued women boldly. I did not fear rebuff, and approached women whom I would never have undertaken if I had not been manic. Out of charity and compassion, some were agreeable. I felt no inconstancy to Jane, only a cheerful lechery. Gus seemed cheerful also, and when a woman and I stood up in my living room, Gus nudged us toward the bedroom. (Sometimes it could be embarrassing: It happened when a neighbor left a casserole.) My sadness was interrupted or replaced only by manic joy, not frequently nor for long periods, the joy usually connected to a love affair. I went to France for two weeks with one woman, to the west of Ireland for a week with another. Some of these relationships sustained me; there were pleasures, there was kindness and affection, but there was also disaffection. My neediness was monumental and I moved from woman to woman, often dismissed when I became difficult. Some of these arrangements were foolish to begin with, and collapsed because the pairing was inherently implausible. I had no judgment. Mania affects the mind as amphetamines do: It quickens everything; it provides new notions accompanied by confidence and incompetence; it removes inhibition and it destroys judgment. The baseball pitcher Dock Ellis told me that a shortstop, using amphetamines, will react more quickly to a ground ball, field it — and then throw it to the wrong base. When mania puts shoes on the wrong feet, it is harmless, but it is not always harmless. I lost three old friends; I misjudged the persons with whom I spoke. But maybe I should not excuse bad judgment by attributing it to mania. ("The devil made me do it" becomes

"It was the adrenal secretions . . .") Thirty years earlier, when my first marriage ended and I lived five years alone, my judgment or behavior was scattery and unreliable. Joining myself to Jane, I became stable and clear-sighted, addicted to her and to work. From time to time during our twenty-three years I understood that her mental and moral clarity was greater than mine. Losing her, I lost the rudder to my ship, and sailed in circles on a dreary sea, able to do nothing except to lament her absence and to hurl myself from woman to woman.

I was not looking for love; love was unthinkable. I wanted sex, only sex, with as many women as possible. The requirement was that no one consider that she was singular in my life. Whenever I kissed someone and proposed bed, I made it a condition that she understand that I would have other girlfriends. I did not want to deceive anyone into believing that I was looking for a wife. And I enjoyed the distracting excitement of multiplicity. What was I looking for? Maybe it was the comfort of touch, of skin, rather than the satisfaction of desire. Or was I cheating on Jane because I was angry at her desertion? Or was it life against death? There were one-night stands, when the question of singularity did not arise. There were affairs that went on for half a year. After five years of casual promiscuity, I went manic again and fell in love with someone ridiculously younger than me. We stayed together for six months, spending a week abroad together. We were *madly* in love. When she broke it off I went into a black melancholy. Grief's house was home only to extremes of emotion.

I knew that my avidity was a response to Jane's death, but I never considered that I was chemically driven until I crashed into despair and rage. This collapse coincided with the end of a brief and pleasant affair, but the woman's defection did not originate the plunge; the onset of my angry depression pushed her away. My mood cycled rapidly, euphoria to dysphoria, rage to self-pity to rage. Mourning turned into melancholia by way of ecstasy. I sat alone in my familiar blue chair, bewildered by sudden and extreme switches from black to gold to black. Nothing like this had happened before. For a short time I was subject to fantasies of murder. At a poetry reading in August of 1996, as I said my poems I suffered images in which I turned a machine gun on the audience. Driving home from the reading, alone in the car, I kept on seeing my listeners crumple and bleed and die. I called Jane's psychiatrist, Dr. Charles Solow, who put me on a psychotropic — and the murderous rages stopped. I remained black, dour, hopeless; I imagined forms of suicide, ingenious and foolproof plots and devices. I could not abide the presence of other people. Two friends visited from another continent, friends by correspondence whom I had never met and wanted to meet. I could barely talk with them. They proposed having dinner with me and I burst into tears and sent them away.

Extremities of depression diminished into a steady gray, week after week of rain. I could get by, do a little work, get through the day wearing a suit of perpetual sadness. I worked every morning on the poems of *Without*. I was aware that I could not trust my judgment about these poems, that I needed other eyes. Always I have relied on the advice of friends, but I have never sought it so systematically as I did with *Without*. When I first assembled a manuscript, I sent it to ten friends. All replied in detail and gave me advice. Some advice contradicted other advice, but I found the letters vastly helpful: I cut, reordered, added, cut; I changed

"I" to "he" in one series of poems. Six months later I sent a heavily revised manuscript to ten more people, none of whom had read it before, so that their responses would not be cluttered by reminiscences of an earlier version. Six months after that, I had a third manuscript, and sent it again to ten people—picking readers who had been most helpful in looking over the first two versions. My readers were old and young, male and female, poets and not-poets. After the third set of responses, I put together the manuscript Houghton Mifflin published as *Without*. I made further revisions when it was reprinted; printings vary.

Two years after Jane's death I was able to dismantle her study, collecting her manuscripts and journals and correspondence for an archive. When we first knew that she would certainly die, she told me that she wanted her papers to go to the University of New Hampshire, which already collected me. Her study was large, with a large closet, in which I found to my surprise one cardboard box for each of her books, each containing folders of drafts for the poems in that book. As I went through the mass of papers on her desk, I found drafts for the new poems that started her posthumous collection, and letters answered or not ever to be answered. Also I found journals, one with a spiral notebook she wrote in as a girl. The oldest began with golly-gee attempts at cheerfulness at the beginning of junior high school. I looked through her notebooks guiltily. I would read a page of text, then shut the book with the sense that I was committing a violation. I read enough of the earliest volumes to encounter a grave change, when the *voulu* good cheer descended into depression. High school was largely a time of misery. When she came to college there were further changes, and she undertook to talk about the men in her life—

and I did not want to read about them. Sometimes she seemed to write about dreams, or some of her anecdotes appeared to be fiction. I did not read enough to discriminate. When I came upon accounts of our life together on the farm, I stopped reading entirely. I feared that I would find the tracks of some anger at me that could never be withdrawn, or even forgotten. I packed the journals into boxes. Other people who had never known Jane could read them in the future when I would not be alive to keep them away. One day librarians from the university showed up with a van and took away the letters, journals, and poems in draft. I had not foreseen that it would devastate me. I wept again as Jane's work left the house of her work that had turned into grief's house. It was as if her dead body again left our threshold.

Friends urged me to travel, but I did not want to go anywhere alone. A poetry reading took me to England, which Jane and I had visited together; I felt restless and out of sorts. I flew to Ireland and did a reading in Dublin, another in Belfast. I took pleasure in gossiping and talking poetry with the poets of Ireland—Michael Longley, Seamus Heaney—but everywhere I traveled I felt incomplete; I was a fragment. Sometimes there were happy moments, even funny ones. In Nebraska to talk poetry at Indian reservations, I took the opportunity to visit Ronda McCormick, who had donated her bone marrow in the attempt to save Jane's life. She and her family welcomed me warmly, fed me well, and as I rose to leave after three hours, Ronda's husband Barry had been delegated to ask me the question the family had been wanting to ask: "Don, do you always wear your shoes on the wrong feet?" I looked down and checked out my shoes. It was true. These were the loafers that Jane had given me our last Christmas, and they were too big. I answered that, of course, *all* poets wore their shoes on the wrong feet.

My days at home lacked purpose. They lacked also the pressure of work. For twenty years at the farm I made a living by writing everything under the sun, from articles for trade publications to anthologies a thousand pages long. The *Ford Times* was a magazine for buyers of Ford cars. For five hundred dollars, I wrote them a thousand-word account of Gertrude Stein's love for their product. I wrote baseball pieces for the *New York Times* and *Sports Illustrated.* I wrote essays for the *Atlantic, Yankee, Harper's,* and *Playboy.* At first I pursued the editors; later I was pursued, editors calling with commissions. One phenomenon I noted: Editors commission you to write again what you have already written. How many times did I get asked to explain the affinity writers feel for baseball? Every time such an essay was commissioned, I made up a new reason. I took pleasure especially in pieces that required interviews with sporting heroes: Carlton Fisk, Kevin McHale, Red Auerbach, Mickey Stanley. It was textbooks that paid the most. I did two essay collections for use in composition classes. I refused at first to do one type of collection—a huge three-genre literature text proposed by several publishers. One day a new publisher proposed such a text, with a large advance—and it was a day when I was worried about money. Several years of hard labor lay ahead of me. Always I worked on poems first, then often on essays or magazine articles, then in the afternoon on compilations including textbooks. On a mantel over a bookcase I displayed the new books, and sometimes there were four in a year—maybe poems, a collection of magazine pieces, a children's book, and a textbook collection of essays.

It was hard work and I loved it. I told myself that I was doing it so that Jane wouldn't have to bag groceries after I died. (She taught middle school as an undergraduate, then college once in New Hampshire. She loathed teaching and frequently said she would rather bag groceries.) But then I laughed at myself: I was claiming a noble purpose—working for Jane and her poetry, working for her widowhood, working for my children's tuitions—while really I was doing exactly what I wanted to do: write and publish, write and publish, write and publish. When Jane died, I discovered that I had been right the first time. Editors called to commission essays and I turned them down. I turned down book editors with notions for new anthologies. I tried half-heartedly to write a children's book, and failed. I entered old age writing poems, the occasional short story, pieces of memoir or nonfiction—avoiding the old moneymakers.

In September, three years after Jane died, I turned seventy, and my children invited me to lunch in Concord. It was a Sunday, and when I went to church I told our minister that I might have to leave the service early because I was meeting my kids. That morning we sang only the first verse of each hymn, and the minister appeared to hurry through the sermon. I was too slow-witted to understand, until he sped through the benediction. I turned to see at the back of the church an enormous birthday cake and heard my friends and cousins belt out "Happy Birthday." The cake was a masterpiece, decorated at its edges with dozens of tiny baseballs and bearing the legend MARK MAGUIRE HIT SIXTY-NINE [the season was not over] BUT DONALD HALL HIT SEVENTY.

Lunch was here in abundance; lunch was waiting in Concord.

The service had been so short that I had time to feast myself with my church friends and thank them before I left for Concord and arrived right on time. For me, to be on time is to be late, and as I pulled into the parking lot at the Centennial Inn, I found my son Andrew nervously pacing up and down. He led me inside to a large basement function room where my children had assembled thirty or forty friends for another surprise party. Even while driving from the church's surprise party to my children's—and even after the fiftieth-birthday surprise party that Jane and Philippa had set up—I had suspected nothing. Robert Bly had flown from Minnesota. Alice and Joyce were there, our friends Liam and Tree, my agent Gerry McCauley, Nan's widower Uncle Dick, Sven Birkerts, David Lehman, Fran McCullough my old editor from Harper and Row, Wes McNair, Charles Simic, Mike and Monique Pride, Galway Kinnell and Bobbie Bristol, Peter Davison my editor at Houghton Mifflin—so many friends from the decades, with husbands and wives. For three hours I ran from group to group. We drank wine; a cook prepared us each a pasta dish according to our tastes. There were speeches, jokes, and little set pieces performed to laughter and applause. At one table, brilliantly dressed, sat five polite grandchildren with Joyce's daughter Elizabeth.

Late in the afternoon the guests began to leave, and the Centennial Inn to clean up. The remaining partyers departed for Philippa's house only a few miles away. Robert Bly asked me to say a Jane poem I was struggling with; I had a problem linking two metaphors, and at my seventieth birthday party Joyce came up with a solution. Then the phone rang and it was Robert Creeley, who had read his poems in Denver the night before. Flying across the country, he was late for the party. He had landed in Manchester, rented a car, and over the phone took directions to Philippa's house. By this time I was exhausted, but happy to see one more old poetry friend. Bob Creeley was exhausted also, and after brief hilarity he went off to his motel while I drove home gaily to enter another decade.

Gaiety was not habitual. Early the next year I spent three months in Manhattan, teaching one night a week. It is the only time I have lived in New York, yet I'm not sure I lived there. Gus never quite understood about living on the eleventh floor, or about elevators, and maybe I didn't either. I didn't feel engaged by my classes. I went to a few poetry readings and one party. Mostly, I stayed alone in the apartment, and gladly returned to Eagle Pond.

❖

As I WRITE THESE WORDS it is many years since Jane died. Now she would be sixty, who is perpetually forty-seven. Still, her absence fills this house. Her handwriting labels jars of spices and lists telephone numbers. I fry Italian sausage in her skillet and boil spaghetti in her kettle and drain it in her colander. I look at her photographed face as I move from room to room. But I no longer scream; rarely do I weep. I drive to her grave only when I introduce her to a visitor. She will remain, filling the air around me like a rainy day, until I lie beside her—which is the prodigy that will keep me safe beside her—but life after Jane has become simply my life, which in old age comes to resemble the life of the only child and solophiliac adolescent. Four or five years ago, my bipolarity subsided. If it was a matter of chemistry, maybe the brain's changes, wrought by stress, rescinded themselves by themselves. I stopped taking psychotropic drugs, and inhabited again a landscape that resembled the countryside before leukemia, with the great difference that I inhabited a solitude of one. I continue to live at Eagle Pond Farm and wake gazing at Mount Kearsarge. I occupy my old skin. For several years now, I have loved a woman who lives an hour away, who can come to me once or twice a week. Gradually over the years, I left grief's house and middle age for the thin air of antiquity's planet.

The Planet of Antiquity

THE NEW MARRIES the old in the sparse air of antiquity's planet. When you are three years old and your socks are falling down, somebody says, "Pull up your socks, Donnie." Then you are twelve, solitary, reading books all day, then twenty-five and a new father, burping your son at two A.M. When you turn forty, divorced, your life is a passage among disasters. Then you marry again, you are happy, you turn sixty, your wife dies. Then you are eighty and your socks fall down again. No one tells you to pull them up.

If I felt like having another cup of coffee—for almost sixty years—impulse became mobility without the intervention of thought; I approached the pot with my empty cup. Now I can't stand up from a chair without being deliberate. I set my hands on the arms of the chair, lean forward a little to shift the poise of my bulk, push up with my hands as frail thigh muscles contort and contract. In triumph I heave myself up. Standing for a moment to consolidate my balance, I pick up the empty cup and lean ahead, putting one foot forward, then another wide of the first. Returning, I set the full coffee cup down, carefully, and lower myself into the chair with arms extended to break the descent.

One lives the thoughtful life on antiquity's planet. How could this happen—the three-year-old, the man at eighty? It is easy, gradual and irreversible, this amble down the lane of old age to-

ward repose's stone city. For my first six decades I occupied myself daydreaming ahead in time—books to write, travels, chores,
pleasures. At eighty you don't waste time planning ten years in
the future. You learn, I suppose, to live in the moment—as you
have been told to do all your life. You live in the moment rising
from a chair. At some point, you will no longer be able to rise
from a chair. So drink your coffee and plan your day, or at least
your next half hour.

Some days your left hip hurts as you jump for the telephone; or,
going down stairs, suddenly your right knee bends in an unprec-
edented direction. It is important not to fall down in a solar system compounded of broken hips. I've become pretty good at falling. I manage to roll, spreading the impact and diminishing it. In
youth and middle age I regularly started to fall—clumsy, tripping
over an ottoman or the dog's leash—but for decades I could right
myself in midair, snapping a foot out to keep myself erect. Feet
no longer snap out. Arms work better, propping oneself against
a wall or a tabletop—but the absence of walls makes trouble. In
New York I was walking with a friend, not looking down, when
the sidewalk on Second Avenue gave way to gravel. My forehead
hit the cement and bled brightly if superficially. It took sixty seconds to get over panic's adrenal hit before I stood with the help of
my friend. A passerby fetched a wad of paper napkins from a café
to stanch the bleeding. Another identified himself as a medical
student and checked me out, staying beside me for five minutes
until I was clearly all right. New York is a city of helpers, at least
for the elderly. Earlier, in Times Square, I had crashed headfirst
over somebody's wheelie suitcase. A woman said, "He needs a
Coke!"—which seemed strange until she returned to press a cold

can against my cheekbone and stop the swelling. A few years ago, while walking to catch a train in Sweden with my love Linda, looking at the train not the pavement, I collided with a pipe sticking up from the ground. I fell rolling and did not even bruise—but Linda hurtled to catch me and achieved wounds on her legs and arms and a hole in her trousers. Probably Linda's psychic bruises were greater. She is almost three decades younger than I am. If she telephones and I do not quickly pick up the phone, her mind endures a vision: I am lying on my back, eyes open, blood drooling from the corner of my mouth.

Imminence of death does not wholly absorb me. Like most people, I dread the dying part, not the being dead. I have no major projects to finish, as I did after the cancers of my sixties. Indeed I want to live, to love, to look at Mount Kearsarge, to write poems, to drink champagne at the weddings of grandchildren, to hold small babies when my grandchildren have children. Not too long ago I had my first stroke, which has left me mostly unscathed. My reaction to the experience surprised me: During the stroke, and an operation to roto-root a clogged carotid, I never felt fear. I felt something like adventure, or at least fascination. The stroke happened at Bennington College, in January of 2001, while I visited a low-residency M.F.A. program. I stayed in a dormitory with writer friends who taught in the program, and ate in the dining room in Commons, reached by a long, steep, awkward staircase. One day I fell on that staircase; later I fell again. The novelist Alice Mattison was with me and shook her head. "This has to be neurological," she said. A day later, I took a nap in the afternoon before a party. When I woke, my left hand and forearm were asleep, and though I shook them the prickling would not go away. I went to the party, came back to bed early, and woke at five A.M. with my whole left side asleep.

Of course I knew what was happening. There was no paralysis, no impediment to motion. Alice Mattison and Betsy Cox, who's also a novelist, were sleeping in rooms across the hall. Before waking them, I would insert my upper plate, because women are not permitted to see me without teeth. In my nightshirt, I knocked on Alice's door, and she woke Betsy, whose car was parked outside. None of us considered calling an ambulance, which would have been sensible. I didn't want to make a fuss. Why was I so calm? Recently, my life had been difficult. Someone I cared for had broken things off, and I had been practicing suicidal thoughts—but I wasn't calm because I wanted to die. Somehow it was *interesting* to have a stroke. I returned to my room and dressed warmly—zero outside—and worked myself into long fleece-lined boots. Betsy and Alice supported me as we descended the stairs and walked over ice in darkness to Betsy's car. Then we could not find the Bennington hospital. We drove around and around, looking for the road sign that would direct us, taking an extra fifteen minutes while I sat in the front seat, gradually warmed by the heater, and noted our predicament: Two novelists frantically try to drive a poet to Emergency while his left side continues its resolute sleep. Finally we found it, and when we walked to Registration I announced that I was having a stroke. Nurses put me to bed and a resident neurologist confirmed my diagnosis and suspected that my right carotid was occluded. An ultrasound made diagnosis secure, and later an MRI showed that the artery was eighty-five percent blocked. Insufficient blood reached the right half of my brain—but as heparin increased blood flow, my left side gradually woke up.

Alice and Betsy returned to the campus and spread the word at breakfast. Alice came back, as well as a multitude of visitors from the program—teachers and students and staff, including dear friends. Liam Rector came calling, who had survived two heart attacks and two unrelated cancers; he took my stroke in stride. Alice sat at the foot of my bed weeping, weeping, weeping. Her tears were interrupted by the arrival of Robert Bly, who was also visiting the program. Ever alert in kindness and care, my oldest friend had stopped at a McDonald's on the way to the hospital, and gifted me with a cheeseburger and French fries. Alice stopped crying.

When I telephoned my assistant Kendel, I avoided small talk. "I'm in the hospital at Bennington," I told her. "I've had a stroke," and allowed her no time for reaction before I started asking her to do this and that. She telephoned my children, who dialed me in my bed and listened to my reassurances. The Bennington neurologist wanted to operate, scooping out the clogged carotid, but I had other thoughts. The Dartmouth-Hitchcock Medical Center, an hour from my house, had been the site of my cancer operations and the place where Jane had spent months with her leukemia. I cherished its nurses and doctors. This hospital would be a comfort because it was near home, nearer my son and daughter and their families. I decided to transfer there by ambulance and have my operation in New Hampshire. I was loaded into a Bennington ambulance with two drivers and a nurse for the journey, two and a half hours, to Lebanon. I arrived at my neurosurgery room later than I was supposed to, with my daughter Philippa waiting for me, and our minister Chuck Higgins. The next day was medical workups and a long MRI. Waiting for Dr. Harbaugh to slice my neck, I was entertained by squads of visitors—Jane's oncologist Letha Mills, her psychiatrist Charles Solow, and nurse after nurse from the blood-cancer ward, where Jane and I had spent much of 1994 and 1995. Nurses sat on the edge of my bed and joked with me. Philippa came again, and Andrew. Kendel came, and I dictated some letters. Late at night, before the operation, a neurology resident visited to read me the dangers that I was undertaking, a necessity both ethical and legal. In the country at large, four percent of patients died on the table during this procedure. Dr. Harbaugh's patients flamed out only two percent of the time. The statistics were encouraging, and I did not regret my ambulance ride, but finally I felt a chill.

The endarterectomy was set for seven A.M., without general anesthesia. Dr. Harbaugh numbed my neck and opened up the right carotid. He avoided using a stent, and I needed to be awake so that I could report any numbness on the left side of my body. I clutched in my left hand a dog's rubber ball with a bell inside, and every few minutes on command I squeezed it and made it jingle. I felt nothing of the incision; I felt no pain over the two hours of action. I was fascinated at the talk of nurses, medical students, and surgeons around me. It was a morning like a green field, and I felt good—attended to by shepherds who spoke softly to each other and to me. Toward the end of the procedure, Dr. Harbaugh lifted in front of me the strange object that had occluded my blood flow—it was whitish, fat as a fountain pen, maybe two inches long. I touched it; it was hard, my self-created self-destroyer. Could I take it home with me? I wanted to keep it under glass, with my collection of small antiquities from Etruscany and Greece and Phoenicia. Dr. Harbaugh refused; these carapaces go to Pathology.

There was little pain even after the anesthetic wore off. I would go home the next day, forbidden to drive a car for a week. For that matter, my car remained at Bennington. By telephone I talked with Liam and Tree, who would drive from Vermont to my house, bringing their car and mine, shortly after Kendel took me back to my house. Through Kendel I arranged for my housekeeper Carole and Steve—Carole's husband is a carpenter and builder—to fix a stout handle into the wall of my shower. It was standing up and walking that concerned me. At home I had a walker that my mother and Jane had used. Kendel would bring it with her when she picked me up. She would get me a cane with four feet. Not worried about dying, I was phobic about falling.

Then I was home again, with food in the refrigerator and help from my housekeeper and my assistant. Carole cleaned and did laundry and tidied. Kendel fetched me the *Globe* each morning until I was permitted to drive the car that Liam and Tree had delivered. To reach the mailbox on Route 4, I used my walker. In the house, the four-footed cane sufficed as I walked with my feet wide apart. Over the next months I drove to Dartmouth-Hitchcock for physical therapy and did exercises at home. When I flew off to do poetry readings, I used a cane that had belonged to my great-grandfather. Waving it in airports, I boarded planes before everybody else. I fell down fairly often—once in a Detroit hotel, twice at a bed-and-breakfast in Tucson. Going down stairs, even one step off a porch, was problematic, because it was hard to hold back my forward hurtle. With a slope or stairs I require a banister. At our house, Jane had installed a railing by the steps up to the porch. First her mother needed it, then Jane, and now me. When I am required to descend stairs without railings—often in auditoriums when I read my poems—I look for someone to give me a hand. Maybe my calmness or amusement during stroke and endarterectomy came from the same place: I was the center of attention—a brave old fellow not afraid to die.

Gradually, on the planet of antiquity, I have become frail. Mostly I don't feel like a codger—but I look into the eyes of others and see that they make out someone *old*. It is an identity, *old*. I feel mild distaste in the eyes of the young. And I feel the same distaste when I look at eighty-five-year-olds in the supermarket. Age is slack and ugly. Should *this* one be driving a car? Will *that* one stop shuffling in the aisle and let me pass? When I see a driver make a turn without a signal, and I glimpse white hair, my response is callous, with the callousness of youth. As it were. What do I want from the genuine young? I suppose I want them to think that I am a vigorous sort—but they are not deceived: When I maneuver and strain to get out of a car, when I hover for a moment standing from a chair, I can look as if I were drunk.

A couple of years back I was driving home, ten-thirty at night, after dinner with Linda and her friend in a restaurant where I had consumed one glass of wine. I was hurrying to get to bed, and speeding along a two-lane New Hampshire highway. I paid no attention to the sign that told me to keep to thirty-five miles an hour. When I became aware of blue lights pulsing behind me, I checked my speedometer: fifty-three. My heart pounded. I pulled off the road to the wide margin and watched the police car settle behind me. I put the car in neutral and reached for my license but in my anxiety failed to pull up the emergency brake. The car drifted a few feet back before I stopped it, and I heard a tap from the horn of the patrol car. I found my license and rooted around in the glove box for my registration. A young man's head leaned down to my open window. "I know I was speeding," I said, "sorry"—and handed over my papers. The head lingered, checking out my face, and then retreated to a car radio.

My heart slowed down its pounding while my criminal record was under scrutiny. When the patrolman returned he asked me to step out of the car, which started adrenaline flowing again. I dreaded being tested on my balance, because my balance since my stroke was poorer than ever. I spoke through the open window. I told him I would get out, but he shouldn't expect me to walk straight: I was an old man and had had a stroke a couple of years ago. The visage leaning toward me showed nothing. He was in his mid-thirties, military-looking, with a crew cut. He was never rude, addressing me always as "sir," polite according to the book, but equally he never showed any interest or compassion; they're not in the book. "Please step out of your vehicle, sir," he said, and "Have you been drinking an alcoholic beverage, sir?" He had smelled my wine. I told him I had had one drink at a restaurant three hours earlier. "Please walk that line, sir." He pointed to a white line at the gutter. I told him I would try—but I was *old.* I walked the straight line with an effort of concentration. I must have looked as if I had just swallowed a quart of vodka. He asked me to stand on one leg. It's been years since I could stand on one leg; I need to sit on my bed in order to put on socks and shoes. The officer continued to run me through sobriety tests, a neurologist's playbook of fingers outstretched, eyes closed, touching nose. "Keep your feet together," said the cop. My physical therapist had advised me to keep them apart. I quoted her without noticeable response.

All the time, I could not believe that he thought I was drunk—which I wasn't. I felt not rage but a sense of the ridiculous. He asked me if I would like to take a Breathalyzer test. I said I'd rather not—which must have sounded like refusal—and that I just wanted to get in the car, drive home, and write the check in the morning for my speeding ticket. He walked away and spoke on his cell phone. Then he approached me. "I am putting you under arrest, sir. This is for your safety and mine, sir," he said, and he pushed me, not roughly, against the side of my car and frisked me for weapons. I told him I was being arrested for being old. "I am not arresting you for being old, sir," he said as he handcuffed me behind my back and stuffed me into the rear seat of his cruiser. I had not been aware that these seats are made of sheet metal, no padding, and that there is scant legroom. The policeman wedged my legs together so that he could close the door. My manacled fists were painful, squeezed between my back and the steel. When my nose itched, over the next hour or so, I could not scratch it. Oddly, I never felt angry, and of course anger would have accomplished nothing. It was one of those moments when you see yourself from far off, freeze-framed for eternity: handcuffed, frail at seventy-odd, stuffed into the back seat of a police cruiser on Route 104 in New Hampton, New Hampshire. Absurd! From time to time I was anxious—suppose the Breathalyzer malfunctioned?—but I felt more amused than panicked. This sense of absurdity was self-preserving, self-protective.

For an hour before we left, my captor kept talking on his cell phone, as telephilic as a teenager. He called for a tow truck. Doubtless he called his chief, and the station in Meredith that would provide the Breathalyzer. Doubtless he called his wife to tell her he would be late. A tow truck lifted away my Honda. *It was happening—it cannot be happening!* After interminable minutes on the phone, my uniformed captor drove me the half hour to the Meredith police station. I told him again that he arrested me for the crime of DWO, driving while old, derived from the well-known crime of DWB: driving while black. He did not appear to be amused: He judged that I was impaired. At the station, he unfolded me from the cruiser's back seat and held on to me as I walked, my balance not improved by having my hands manacled behind me. Inside the building he unlocked the cuffs, and I was grateful to have my hands back. He introduced me to the sergeant who would administer the Breathalyzer, and who explained the procedure. After some consultation between officers I was permitted to urinate, under observation. Did they think I would climb out a window? Otherwise, while the Breathalyzer warmed up, I was required to sit in a chair. I am a pacer, and I wanted to pace. No pacing was allowed. I felt my thigh muscles twitch. My mind remained calm, but my body was not calm. I looked over my shoulder through the open door of a small jail cell, an unpadded ledge for sleeping on. I wondered what damage my arrest was doing to my body. I am diabetic, and adrenaline increases sugar.

We didn't have much to talk about. The baseball season, which occupies me six months a year, had not begun, but I tried talking about the Red Sox. It was a subject on which I am well informed, but neither of the officers seemed to share my obsession. I knew enough not to bring up the war in Iraq, but a bumper sticker had already revealed my opinion: *Dean.* I wondered if *Dean* contributed to my crime. Most of the time we sat in silence. I was thirsty, but I was not permitted a glass of water. When the machine was ready, the sergeant told me how to breathe into it, and then consulted the figures. I scored zero on the Breathalyzer. I took the test again and scored zero again. I was triumphant. I shook the hand of the arresting officer. He and the sergeant spoke quietly together, and I saw them tear up the forms the patrolman had filled out. I was not charged with speeding—I suppose I had done enough time—but I received no other apology.

My officer and I walked out of the police station, back to the squad car. The back seat was less difficult without handcuffs, but it was still hard. I was almost an hour from my house, but only half an hour from my car. I looked forward to resuming my drive home. When I told the policeman that I would be certain not to speed when I drove home, he let me know, with some awkwardness, that I would not be driving home. At first he remained passive—I would be driven home—and he tried to set up a scheme whereby the police from one town would ferry me to a police station farther along, each ride interrupted by waiting for the next car. Why could I not drive home? "You know I scored zero." He was evasive. He had judged me impaired. Perhaps I was on some other drug—he assured me that he knew I wasn't—or some medication. I repeated that I was guilty of DWO. Why, really, wasn't I allowed to drive? Maybe there could have been liability if he let me drive and I had an accident.

There were more phone calls. He rendezvoused with another police car in a dark parking lot. I was not transferred. At some point he cleared off the front seat beside him and permitted me the luxury of upholstery, a relief after the steely back seat. When we reached the Bristol police department, my protector called the Danbury police, trying to get them to drive to Bristol and take me the rest of the way home, but the Danbury cars were busy. My patrolman sighed and stood and told me he would drive me all the way home. Good. I could be home in twenty-five minutes. I told him I could kiss him—and my gratitude seemed to make him nervous. He said that shaking hands would do just fine.

I directed him down 104 to Danbury where it runs into Route 4, and five miles south to my house. He pulled into my U-shaped driveway and I unloosed my seat belt. "Come on in," I said, "and have a beer." Something like a smile brushed across his face for the first time. "Not until I get home," he said. I went inside and had a beer for both of us. I telephoned Linda, who would be staying up talking with her friend, and told her my adventure. Her friend remarked that I would have enjoyed it more had it been Linda handcuffing me.

❖

In the morning Kendel drove me to the lot where they had towed my car, and I was permitted to buy it back for the towing fee. It's remarkable that I never fell down while being handcuffed and put through my neurological paces. In general, my limbs work better than they might. For a while my right hip pained me when I walked more than fifty yards. Glucosamine appears to have banished hip pain. Or maybe it just went away. For a year or so I suffered from a sore neck, with pains shuttling between my neck and the top of my shoulder—mostly on my right side, then shifting over to my left. Because I started sleep on one side or the other, I studied which side was most amenable to unconsciousness. Then it stopped; for several years now I have had no neck pain. I had assumed that when you are old and discover a pain, it will only get worse. Not so. But one can expect a new pain to replace the departed one. My most debilitating illnesses have occurred more recently. The autumn of 2005 was dreadful, with overwhelming fatigue together with difficulty in sleeping at night and a gradual diminishing of appetite. I would sleep a few hours, with pills, and wake at six feeling tired. By eight-thirty A.M. I felt horribly fatigued, wearing a suit of ice, hardly able to read and wholly unable to write. Thus I spent October, November, and December.

At first I thought this fatigue was the Republican Party's fault like everything else. The NEA had asked me to the National Book Festival late in September, and it sounded like a good thing, sponsored by the Library of Congress. Slowly I learned details. It would begin with a black-tie dinner at the library on Friday night, followed by next morning's breakfast in the White House, then readings in a tent on the Mall. First I asked if George W. Bush would be present, an unlikely thought but essential information. If there was a chance I might be expected to shake our president's hand, I would not attend. He would not be present, so I felt safe. Friday night began with a series of speakers, and I understood that the festival was less about literature than about literacy; everyone speaking was for literacy. Laura Bush, the former school librarian, spoke in favor of books, and the applause was monumental. I began to wonder where I was. At dinner I found out. Like the other writers invited, I was one writer at a table with seven Republicans, apparently contributors to the party. These people gave thousands; they were not the givers of millions, who slept in the Lincoln Bedroom. The woman on my right—who never spoke to me after ascertaining that I was a poet; my hair was long and uncombed—was married to a silver-haired senator from Texas named Cornyn, whom I had never heard of. I talked with the woman on my left, who spotted me instantly as a northeastern liberal. She was in fact from Massachusetts and had started life as a Democrat, but "the Democrats left us" when Ronald Reagan beat Jimmy Carter. She was lively and strong-willed, and her husband "was AT&T," as she put it. The dinner was for Republican loyalists, and I didn't belong at the table. I'd been at such dinners for donors before, notably at the Boston Public Library, which also puts one writer at every table. The other guests are the women who support the library and their silent husbands who support them. At the last one I attended, a grumpy man across the table addressed me: "What do you write about?" "Love, death, and New Hampshire," I told him—and briefly considered that I had stumbled on a title for my selected poems.

Nothing witty occurred to me this Washington night. I remember that the food was good but I had no appetite, and excused myself at the advent of dessert. The next morning Linda and I were due at the White House for breakfast at seven-thirty. We arose at six, and alighted early in back of the White House. We sat in an amphitheater while Mrs. Bush addressed us again. Dikembe Mutombo and other basketball stars—the NBA is in favor of reading—took a small part in the program. Then we departed for breakfast, which was a buffet. The lines were interminable and I ate nothing. The rooms on this floor were opulent, but there was no bathroom. To use a bathroom, I was accompanied by a uniformed soldier and delivered to a Secret Service man who ran the elevator—because it could go up one floor into the Residence. Never was a breakfast piss so honored.

When we got away, we were taken with the other writers and literary mavens by bus to the Mall where there were separate tents for fiction and poetry. At the Mall, people were parading in protest against the war in Iraq, and the police had blocked off the street adjacent. I wanted to be part of the protest and not someone who had just visited the White House for breakfast. I was scheduled to read my own things and Walt Whitman as well—for Whitman's 150th birthday—and I was so tired that I could not stand up while reading. Dana Gioia, of the National Endowment for the Arts, arranged the platform so that I could read sitting down, and I did my reading with half the voice that I normally produce. When I read Whitman's "Out of the Cradle Endlessly Rocking," I did not know whether I could get through it. I finished it, and felt finished, but then I had to sit in a small adjacent tent to sign books. There was a Library of Congress staffer assigned to look after me, who commandeered a golf cart to take me to a taxi and the bliss of my bed in the motel. But I lay on the bed twitching and miserable, too exhausted to nap. We had supper in the room, and I slept a restless night. In the morning Linda walked a few blocks to the National Gallery and the Hirshhorn while I stayed in bed.

When I flew home the fatigue persisted, a monumental tiredness that allowed no respite. I was not able to write, not poems and not memoir. I made an appointment with my doctor and had blood drawn for tests. When I saw him the blood work showed nothing, but I worried about my continual fatigue and inability to work. My doctor smiled and pronounced, "You are depressed." Immediately I agreed with him. Chronic fatigue, sleeplessness, inability to work . . . Surely I was depressed. He wrote me a prescription for Paxil. After taking it, I felt immediately anxious. I looked up the possible side effects of Paxil and anxiety was one of them. Then I was suddenly unable to urinate. At ten-thirty one night I had been trying to piss for five hours and it became painful. Kendel took me to Emergency at the New London Hospital and they fitted me with a catheter. At home I reread the side effects of Paxil and found "urinary retention" listed. I stopped taking Paxil. In a week I made an appointment at Dartmouth-Hitchcock, where I had undergone annual appointments with Urology. A nurse removed the catheter and asked me to walk around for two hours to see if I could piss by myself. I knew I couldn't walk more than twenty minutes at a time, but I did the best I could. When I returned I could not pee. The nurse departed for a moment to consult with a resident, who popped his head in and told me that the nurse would educate me in self-catheterization. Thus I went home with my equipment, told to self-catheterize four times a day for a month. Wash hands; put slippery goo on long tube; insert tube in penis and push, past a hurting prostate, more than a foot into the bladder until urine bubbles forth; then extract tube and wash it and set it to dry. From the first, I was urinating normally in between procedures, but I do what I am told, so I continued self-catheterizing. My doctor talked to a urologist at Dartmouth-Hitchcock and relayed official permission to stop it.

Urination remained normal, but I went on suffering from

massive, debilitating fatigue. November was worse than October, December than November. I took sleeping pills at night and slept four or five hours. I took sleeping pills by day in order to nap. At night I drank wine in order to feel sleepy, but still lay awake for a couple of hours before sagging into sleep. Awake, I could do nothing, and became convinced that I would never write again. I continued to ascribe my troubles to depression. Jane's psychiatrist Dr. Solow answered my call and visited, and I went back on an antidepressant that I had used before. I was indeed depressed—but its origins were physical. In November, with nothing improved and my appetite disappeared, I had to force myself to eat a half sandwich. On New Year's Eve Linda and I went to our favorite restaurant simply because it was Saturday night, and discovered that for the holiday the restaurant had substituted a prix fixe instead of the usual menu. The food would be glorious and ample—starters, salad, main dish, dessert—and I could eat nothing but one cup of lobster bisque. I saw my doctor again and had blood work again. This time, the tests showed trouble with my electrolytes, in particular a deficiency of sodium, probably caused by diuretics. There was malfunction in my kidneys and malnourishment and deficiency in vitamins and minerals. My doctor wanted me to enter Concord Hospital, and the next day booked me in. All my medications were changed. Some of my blood pressure medicines, and medicine for diabetes, were diuretic, and because of swollen ankles I had also been taking a pure diuretic. Doctors were puzzled that I had not had seizures, my sodium was so low.

In the hospital, my sodium stopped its plunge and began to restore itself. After five days, I could no longer stay in the hospital, because of Medicare and insurance rules. The doctors wanted me to enter a nursing facility, but I wanted to go home, and I prevailed. It was a mistake. I went home and my legs were weak and my balance still bad. One night I woke at midnight and dashed to the bathroom, forgetting my walker or cane. As I left the bathroom I fell on my back and I could not stand up. I dragged myself, on my back, to my bedroom where there was a telephone, but I knocked it down and the door closed behind me. I lay in the darkness unable to find the phone, or turn on a light, or stand up. I spent the night on my back on the floor of my bedroom. At six-fifteen I heard Kendel in the house, bringing me my newspaper (I was timid about driving to the store), and when she discovered me supine, she dialed 911. Shortly, three strong young men from the Wilmot Fast Squad lifted me up. The phone rang and it was Linda. "Residence of Donald Hall," Kendel's voice told her—but I was able to talk to her and prove that I was not dead.

The next day I acquired a Lifeline button to wear around my neck and made arrangements to have visiting nurses. That night my son Andrew drove up and stayed with me. I managed to fall one time even while using my walker. My doctor understood that I needed to go into a nursing facility to do PT and OT and learn how to stand from a chair and walk without falling down. First I needed to go back to the hospital for three days—three midnights, by Medicare rules—before I could be admitted to a facility. Andrew delivered me to Emergency, and three days later I entered Pleasant View, where I spent two weeks and two days. At first I could not go to the bathroom without a walker and an aide in attendance. After a week I used a cane and finally was free to walk. My roommate was 101 years old and not talkative.

I had many visitors: my children, Linda, my friends—and doctors. When I was strong enough to go home, the visiting nurse set me up with PT, Meals on Wheels, and the nurse herself, who drew blood to confirm that my sodium remained normal. After two weeks I could travel on my own, and drove, and even worked a little on prose and poetry. I was not tired all the time. I took a nap midday as I had done for fifty years. I began again to revise this prose memoir and a few poems—verses about debilitating fatigue, now that I was no longer fatigued. I looked forward to the publication of my new selected poems, *White Apples and the Taste of Stone.*

Then on May 30, 2006—not long after the new book appeared—I had a fax from the Library of Congress: I was appointed Poet Laureate of the United States, if I chose to accept the position. Linda was with me when it arrived, and was so excited—and I was so touched by her excitement—that I could not think about turning it down. Public announcement followed on June 12—and I was dumbfounded by the response. The telephone rang all day every day: telephone interviews, arrangements for personal interviews, radio, television . . . I did two NPR interviews, probably the next day, at the New Hampshire NPR station. New England Cable Television arranged a visit, and the George Stephanopoulos show. (Typically, these shows recorded four hours in order to broadcast four minutes.) PBS arrived, Jeffrey Brown to interview me for the *NewsHour.* The *Los Angeles Times* sent a reporter to the house, and the New Hampshire *Concord Monitor.* The *Wall Street Journal* did an editorial as well as an interview. The *Boston Globe* ran an editorial. *Sports Illustrated* sent a reporter and ran a whole page. (I'd written two books on baseball, many magazine pieces, and a few poems.) The *New York Times* called me a well-known scourge of the religious right, about which I don't believe I have ever uttered a word. Someone must have remembered that when I was on the council of the National Endowment for the Arts, I kept defending the First Amendment, which meant that I approved of sexual content in the arts—called pornography by the far right.

It was my Warholian fifteen minutes, and it lasted well into August. I signed on with an agreeable and resourceful lecture agent, Alison Granucci. My New Hampshire neighbors celebrated me, renting space in Camp Kenwood across Eagle Pond. They invited dozens of local friends, and literary friends who attended from a distance and who made little speeches about me. I read some poems. My daughter was there with my granddaughter Abigail. Then at the end of September, I returned to the National Book Festival, this time avoiding the black-tie Republican dinner and breakfast at the White House. Then I segued to the Library of Congress, and radio shows multiplied again, more than I can remember—and the whole laureate year elapsed in a blur of activity. Officially, it began with an inaugural reading at the library in October. Linda was with me in Washington and for all my travels that year, providing comfort and love. My children flew down for the occasion from New England, which pleased me no end—as they pleased me by the tender attention they administered when I was sick. These beneficences sustain me, in the thin air of antiquity's planet, where I survive to love and write poems as long as I can.